Writing Across the Curriculum

Writing Across the Curriculum
All Teachers Teach Writing

Shelley S. Peterson

PORTAGE & MAIN PRESS

Portage & Main Press acknowledges the financial support of the Government of Canada through the Book Publishing Industry Development Program (BPIDP) for our publishing activities.

Printed and bound in Canada by Friesens

Library and Archives Canada Cataloguing in Publication

Peterson, Shelley

    Writing across the curriculum : all teachers teach writing/Shelley S.

Peterson.—Rev ed.

Includes bibliographical references.

ISBN 978-1-55379-177-5

    1. English language—Composition and exercises—Study and teaching

(Elementary). 2. Language arts—Correlation with content subjects.

I. Title.

LB1576.P48 2008   372.62'3044   C2008-903185-7

PORTAGE & MAIN PRESS

100 – 318 McDermot Ave.
Winnipeg, MB
Canada R3A 0A2
Tel: 204-987-3500
Toll-free: 1-800-667-9673
Toll-free fax: 1-866-734-8477
Email: books@pandmpress.com
www.pandmpress.com

Contents

Chapter 4: Writing Non-Narrative Across the Curriculum   21

Chapter 5: Writing Poetry Across the Curriculum   29

Chapter 6: Writing Narrative Across the Curriculum   39

Chapter 7: Teaching Writing Conventions Across the Curriculum   51

Chapter 8: Teaching Writing as More than Words on a Page: Using Computers and Multimedia   57

Foreword

At some point during our teacher training, all of us studied the various learning theories propounded by educational psychologists—behaviorism, developmental stage theory, cognitive science, information processing, schema theory, and others. And we learned that all these different models of learning, which are otherwise quite contradictory and even antagonistic, agree on one thing: in order for learners to access, comprehend, and retain information, they need to act upon it. "Sit 'n git," a name we might well give to traditional, presentational schooling, simply doesn't work. A curriculum in which we merely mention ideas, facts, and concepts has no staying power for students.

One way to ensure that students act upon content is to have them write about it. But, in order to have power, this writing must be in students' own words—they have to make it their own. Copying down lines or paragraphs just isn't active enough. And even taking notes while being lectured doesn't count as taking mental action—just think of how many times you've turned yourself into a human transcribing machine, mechanically taking down words without taking in the attached ideas.

So kids need lots of "real" writing across the curriculum. And hence today's battle cry: "Every teacher a teacher of writing!"

But wait a minute. This past year I have been teaching grade-6 science and social studies in New Mexico. My content area colleagues and I might have a few questions about this bandwagon of writing to learn. First of all, where are we supposed to find the class time to invite students to write extensively about our subjects? After all, there is so much material to be covered, so many facts and concepts to be taught. And, while we are talking about it, we content people were never trained as teachers of writing in the first place. Shouldn't this be someone else's job? Maybe the junior teachers? And even if, out of pure goodwill, we decided to find the time and do more writing in our subjects, exactly what are we supposed to do or say or assign?

Just as we find ourselves marinating in all these worries, along comes Shelley Peterson to sort it all out: the why, the what, the when, and the how of content area writing. She understands the lives we are living, knows our jammed schedules, realizes how overstuffed the curriculum is, honours the constraints we live with—and then she makes it looks easy to infuse our teaching with smart, engaging writing activities that deepen kids' thinking about the subjects we teach.

With my own class this year, I have been doing many of the same activities Shelley advocates in this book, and so I can testify from immediate experience: this stuff really works. Not only do these content area writing activities deepen kids' knowledge and retention of information, but they also invite enthusiasm about learning. As I write this in June, my 24 kids have just scattered off to middle schools around the city, bringing with them tools for thinking though writing that I know will serve them well for years to come. Because they have connected to both writing and the subject areas so powerfully, they are not just able to write, but are also eager to do so. They're not just compliant about learning the required subjects as they move through the grades, but they are also alive with curiosity, with burning questions and emerging specialties in subjects across the curriculum. I know that Jose, Tanya, and Nayetzy will continue to learn and write about animal extinction; that Daniel and Devin will author further pieces about nuclear weapons and the threats they pose to our world. And I know that Ashley, Diego, and Jessica will write more on the scientific topics—and ultimately, careers—they seek.

Dear reader, you have a treat ahead. Shelley is about to surprise you with some of her great ideas, such as:

- today's kids are the most experienced authors we have ever taught
- you can use poetry to teach math, science, and social studies
- teachers must write in front of their students, demonstrating how we think when we, as proficient adults, compose

And Shelley will guide you all the way along with:

- detailed mini-lessons that show you exactly how to use writing as a tool of teaching and learning all across the curriculum
- ways to help students find content area related writing topics they can really own—and how to find the just-right genres to carry their message
- great examples of real students' work you can use to prime the pump with your own kids
- smart and practical guidance on using the Internet as a writing resource
- a huge appendix filled with all kind of helpful information: handouts, tools, classroom forms, assessment rubrics and more
- various bibliographies that lead to both student and adult texts that can enrich our knowledge

One especially important feature of Peterson's book is her extensive treatment of what we sometimes call *formal* or *public* writing. While many other professional books, including my own, cover the kind of short, spontaneous writing-to-learn strategies that teachers can use to deepen students' engagement before, during, and after lessons (admit slips, exit slips, written conversations, silent discussions, writing breaks, and so on), Shelley also focuses on a family of more lengthy and challenging writing activities that require of students careful planning, deep thinking, and thorough editing, with a wider audience in mind.

This is a book that promises plenty—and delivers extra. Enjoy!

Harvey Daniels

> *I write because I don't know what I think until I read what I say.*
>
> —Flannery O'Connor (in Murray)

Writing and Learning Across the Curriculum

Chapter 1

THE VALUE OF WRITING ACROSS THE CURRICULUM

Many of you teach it all. You paddle alongside your students down a river of reading, writing, viewing, listening, and speaking, across the lake of Greece, an ancient civilization, through the stream of force and motion, and you consider countless other topics within the grade-level curriculum. Across all these subject areas, you probably find that there is so much for students to learn and so little time in the school day for them to do the learning. The challenge is not in the amount of material that there is to teach—it can be rather exciting, really—but rather in finding a way to accomplish everything within the classroom schedule. Meeting this challenge could take the form of integrating content and skills like writing across subject areas.

Some of you specialize in and teach one subject area to a large number of students. Whether you teach it all or whether you specialize, you probably already know the value of writing in content areas. Yet, with the limited time you have to teach the concepts, writing can seem like an add-on, just one more thing to add to the long list of things you need to achieve in a day. Finding time for students to write is a challenge. And then finding time to assess and grade all the writing is another challenge altogether. You envision the stacks of papers from the hundreds of students you teach each week, and the idea of having students write more can be daunting. This book is intended for those teachers who teach language arts and also for those teachers who are specialists in history, geography, math, science, health, French, and so on. You will find ideas for teaching and assessing writing in content areas, ideas that take into account the challenges of your teaching context and the limits to your time.

WHY IS THIS BOOK IMPORTANT?

In a world where information grows at dazzling rates and is available from a multitude of sources, a person's ability to make sense of information is an ever-increasing challenge. To communicate what is learned is important in contemporary life and in what we imagine life might be for our students when they become adults. The importance of writing in content areas is clearly stated in new provincial and state guidelines for school curricula at all levels.

It is my belief, and the point of this book, that we need to make sure that our students learn to communicate through writing, not just in language arts classes but also in content areas. Science, social studies, and health, for example, provide students with real-life questions and ideas to explore. Content area topics also provide students with opportunities to hone the questioning, problem-solving, and organization skills that contribute to good writing.

Students do not have to be in language arts classes to play with the words, rhymes, and rhythms of poetry, or to develop dialogue for a play. They can do all these things while writing about science concepts or historical facts, for example. As students are learning about concepts within content area subjects, they can also be developing as writers. The various content areas can introduce students to genres in writing as they are used in real-life contexts. For example, when students read about how to create a pulley system in their science class, they see how an explanation is written and can use it as a model for their own writing. Students who are learning about municipal government in social studies might communicate that learning by writing letters to the editor of a local newspaper.

I have found that students generally show great enthusiasm for writing brochures, narratives, and poems, whereas completing short-answer and note-taking assignments generate far less interest. Researchers Deborah Brandt and Harvey Graff (2005), who look at workplace literacy skills, tell us that good writing skills are becoming, more than ever before, critically important in a broad range of work environments. Our students' success in the workplace will depend on being able to gather and synthesize information from a number of sources (such as websites, books, articles, interviews, and CDs) and communicate it to others. By integrating writing instruction into content areas, we can help students develop an attitude that effective writing skills are an important part of many of their daily activities and will be, increasingly so, in their future endeavours.

This book is based on the view that the process of writing helps learners think more deeply about ideas and information that they encounter when reading, listening, viewing, and moving about their worlds, which in turn leads to a fuller understanding of the information, than were they not to write about them. I call this *discovery writing*. I am referring to the writing of stories, essays, poems, or any whole piece of writing for which students have some control over the format, topic, purpose, and audience. The act of writing helps students make sense of the rolling, backtracking highway of thoughts running through their heads. The written words, phrases, sentences, and paragraphs give these thoughts some shape and form. As Flannery O'Connor expresses in the quote at the beginning of this chapter, the very act of searching for words and then rubbing them up against each other creates spaces for new understandings to emerge. Janet Emig (1983) explains that, in order to write, students' thoughts have to slow down so that their hands can capture them. Slowing down "allows for surprise, time for the unexpected to intrude and even take over" (p. 112). Discovery and deep thinking rarely happen when students are asked to fill in blanks, copy notes from a blackboard, or provide short answers to questions. Although these types of cryptic writing can be helpful for gathering information that will aid them in composing a more sustained piece of writing later on, they generally do not lend themselves to wild sparks of creativity or deep pools of focused thought. Katie Wood Ray (2001) writes that short answers or learning-log entries are "a piece of cake compared to developing an argument convincingly for an audience" (p. 21); they are not as demanding as the type of writing I call discovery writing.

Exciting new ideas and deeper understandings are not likely to leap out at students if they are given just a few periods in a content area to plan, write, revise, and edit their writing in that area. Rather, writing instruction could begin as a content area unit begins and continue throughout the unit, taking up 15 to 20 minutes of each class throughout the unit. Or it could happen in blocks, when teachers might devote a number of content classes to just writing. Teachers may choose to use the time set aside in language arts classes for writers workshops to work on content area writing. In chapter 2, I address the issue of finding time to dedicate to writing.

When we integrate writing into content areas, there are two main goals— first to reinforce the concepts, and, second to help improve students' writing abilities. Students write in any subject area and in the process explore their worlds and come to know more about themselves. Through discovery writing, students learn to expand their sense of who they are and learn about all that life has to offer. The time devoted to writing has greater benefits than can be captured in any list of curriculum objectives in any particular subject area.

WHAT TO CONSIDER IN CONTENT AREA WRITING

There are a number of questions to consider when you ask students to do more than simply supply answers to questions in content classes. For example: How much freedom should students have to choose the format, genre, topic, and tone? How much emphasis should be placed on basic writing conventions? What should teachers assess? Each of these questions could generate hours of interesting discussion among educators.

How Much Freedom Should We Allow?

When we start to think about having students write in content areas, many of us recall images from our own school years—writing a report on a particular country in social studies class or writing about an animal in science class, for example. But content area writing can be made so much more interesting than that. Consider, for example, the possibility that students might write on any topic they choose, using whatever genre and tone that they think is appropriate for their topic. Students could use their imaginations to incorporate their own knowledge bases and interests with what they have learned in the unit. The only

Leonora, a grade-8 science teacher, says that her students' narrative writing about pulleys helped them to "think about what potential things can happen outside the class lesson." One of her students agreed, saying, "It feels like it pays off more when you finish because it seems like you did more." On top of learning more, another student found the experience enjoyable: "It was kind of easier to learn because she put it in a way that was fun for us."

constraint would be that students must write about the topic of the particular unit of study. Students could write in any genre they wanted: narrative, non-narrative, poetry, cartoon, for example. They would be free to write in whatever way they found personally meaningful and enjoyable.

Some teachers might argue that students could lose ownership of their writing when they write in content areas; they might become more intent on demonstrating their content area knowledge than of how they are writing. These teachers would be concerned that, if the teacher introduced a content area writing task, students would have less choice in what they wrote about in a writers workshop. Yet, my experience with grade-6 and grade-8 science students shows that students appreciate having some parameters set on their writing. It helps them focus their writing.

The students I observed carrying out discovery writing in Leonora's grade-8 class thought first about what they wanted to write. In the backs of their minds, they remembered that they had to show what they knew about the science concepts. But, foremost in their minds, just as in a writers' workshop, the students' main concerns were making sure that they could fit in all they wanted to say and imagining their audience's response. In these classes, students no longer struggled to find a topic for their writing as students so often do in open-choice writers workshops. With a well-defined topic already in place, students have a starting point from which to imagine and create. Researchers such as Timothy Lensmire (1994), Margaret Finders (1997), Brett Elizabeth Blake (1997), and myself (Peterson 2003) question how "free" the free-choice writing in open-choice writers workshop really is. In our research, we found that the assumptions and values of the classroom social network sometimes constrain students' choices of topic. I observed in my research that students try to stay within the parameters of what their peers consider acceptable, and they often write using stereotypical views of gender and social class. I also observed that peers ridiculed the one student who voluntarily decided to go against peer expectations in choosing his or her own topic for writing. In my research, students tended to align their writing with what their peers expected in order to avoid social embarrassment. I believe that the notion of free choice of topic is illusory, in some respects, as all writers are aware of the social consequences that go along with taking perspectives or writing about topics that are outside the mainstream. When teachers create some boundaries for students' writing choices in content areas, they implicitly give students permission to try something that might go against prevailing assumptions within the peer social network. Peers are not likely to ridicule students who try something new in writing if the student is writing according to expectations set by the teacher.

How Much Emphasis Should We Place on Basic Writing Conventions?

Another consideration in content area writing is the degree of attention that teachers should pay to the basic writing conventions of spelling, punctuation, and grammar. Many students spend countless hours blogging, emailing, and text messaging. Compared to generations past, students now have much more opportunity in their daily lives to write. And they appear to enjoy this socially oriented writing. But the problem with these types of electronic communication is that the writing does not follow basic conventions. It is informal, shortened, and contains phonetic spellings of words, symbols with meanings that most teachers do not understand, and sentence structures that follow "technostandards." Clearly, students nowadays write more than previous generations did, but they write in a different way. I believe that we as teachers need to guide students so that they recognize that the informality of electronic communication is not appropriate in all contexts. The more formal contexts require that they know the basic writing conventions (tone, spelling, grammar, and punctuation). This means that reinforcing appropriate writing conventions is as necessary in science classes as it is in language arts classes. It is important that students get the message that effective communication is important in every part of their world—with their friends and family, and in school.

What Should Teachers Assess?

Should teachers assess their students' knowledge of the content area or quality of writing? Some teachers might argue against assessing basic writing skills when marking content writing, for fear that it will overshadow students' understanding of the concepts. They would suggest that students' grades should reflect their understanding of the concepts, not their writing skills. I believe, however, that it benefits students if teachers pay attention to developing students' writing skills; it is crucial that students be able to communicate their content knowledge. We need to help students understand that it is not just the learning of ideas that is important but also how they communicate those ideas. The assessment checklists in BLMs 9.2, 9.3, 9.4, and 9.5 are designed to help address this issue. They stress content knowledge demonstrated in the writing, but they also assess features of writing, such as organization, style, and basic conventions.

HOW TO USE THIS BOOK

Several chapters in this book contain mini-lessons, which are designed to help you teach specific concepts and ways of writing. I have used these mini-lessons in various contexts across the grades. You may adapt them to any curriculum topic you teach. I have prepared a number of blackline masters (BLMs), which serve to complement the information in the text. Use them if you plan to teach mini-lessons and to assess your students' writing. Feel free to photocopy these for use in your classrooms. They are referred to throughout by BLM number and are found at the end of the book.

WORKS CITED

Blake, B.E. *She Say, He Say: Urban Girls Write their Lives.* Albany, NY: SUNY Press, 1997.

Brandt, D., and H. Graff. *Continuing the Conversation on Literacy Past, Present and Future.* NCTEAR Midwinter Conference. Columbus, OH: February, 2005.

Emig, J. "Hand, Eye, Brain: Some 'Basics' in the Writing Process." In J. Emig, D. Goswami, and M. Butler (eds.), *The Web of Meaning: Essays on Writing, Teaching, Learning and Thinking*, 109–121. Upper Montclair, NJ: Boynton/Cook Publishers, 1983.

Finders, M.J. *Just Girls: Hidden Literacies and Life in Junior High*. Urbana, IL: NCTE, 1997.

Lensmire, T. *When Children Write: Critical Re-Visions of the Writing Workshop*. New York: Teachers College Press, 1994.

Murray, D. *Shop Talk: Learning to Write with Writers*. Portsmouth, NH: Heinemann, 1990.

Peterson, S. "Gender Meanings in Grade Eight Students' Talk about Classroom Narrative Writing." *Gender and Education* 14.4 (2003), 351–366.

Wood Ray, K. *The Writing Workshop: Working through the Hard Parts (and They're All Hard Parts)*. Urbana, IL: NCTE, 2001.

Organizing Classrooms for Writing in Content Areas

Chapter 2

FINDING A PLACE FOR WRITING IN CONTENT AREA CLASSES

Think about the last science, social studies, health, music, art, or mathematics unit you taught. Were students involved in hands-on activities with concrete materials? Did they hear guest speakers? Did they go on field trips? Did they consult the Internet, books, magazines, newspapers, or other print sources and take notes on what they learned? Did they discuss problems or questions in small groups? Did they demonstrate their learning by creating a visual, oral, or written products? Did they learn how to improve their writing in mini-lessons that you taught and by having conferences with you and their peers? Most likely, you can answer yes to all these questions, except, perhaps, for the final one. In this chapter, I present plans and ways of organizing content area classes that provide support for students in their content learning as well as in their writing development. When you are integrating writing into content areas, your planning can often be complicated because you are juggling content area objectives and writing objectives. This chapter helps you with the juggling.

The list on page 8 is a useful tool for integrating writing into the curriculum. You can teach content area curriculum at the same time as you are developing students' writing abilities. See BLM 2.1 for a template that you can use in your own unit planning. And see appendix A for examples that show how this planning framework might be used in science, social studies, and health classes.

When you are planning, the content objectives will likely come from the content area curriculum that you teach. The writing objectives and assessment criteria can come from both the language arts curriculum and from previous assessments of your students' writing. Focus the mini-lessons on elements of writing, such as how to use dialogue in fiction writing, how to support the main point with examples and details in non-narrative writing, or how to use specific words in poetry writing. Students may have demonstrated in their previous writing that they had difficulty with these elements, or the curriculum may indicate that these are important elements for students to master.

FRAMEWORK FOR INTEGRATING WRITING ACROSS THE CURRICULUM

1. Identify the content area learning objectives and the writing objectives that will serve as the focus for students' learning.

2. Develop activities to help students gather and organize the information associated with the learning objectives. These activities can include concrete experiences, such as hands-on activities with manipulatives, experiments, interviews, reading print and non-print texts, drawing, painting, sculpting, field trips; the possibilities are as vast as your imagination allows.

3. Provide choice for students as they select their writing formats, and encourage them to think about the content within the subject area. Introduce students to a range of formats that they can use for their writing. Be sure to include narrative, non-narrative, and poetry. These all work well for any content area.

4. Allow time for students to interact with peers and to work independently to gather and organize information, write, revise and discover, edit, and communicate their learning to an audience.

5. Teach mini-lessons that address the original objectives and address the new objectives that arise as students engage in learning experiences.

6. If possible, schedule time for one-on-one student-teacher conferences.

7. Determine how students will share their writing with a wider audience.

When students are writing in any subject area, it is important that you schedule writing time as often as possible during the week. If you are teaching language arts as well as content areas, you can integrate the content area writing assignments with the other writing in writers workshop. The mini-lessons, conferencing, and sharing of writing (in small groups, in pairs, or as a class) can take place during language arts classes or content area classes. The writing that you assign for content area classes can be woven into the fabric of the writers workshop. During the time allotted for writing, students can be working on their free-choice writing or on their content area writing. They may need guidance in planning their time so that they can meet the deadlines for their content area writing.

It is possible for a piece of writing from a content area class to be only one of a number of pieces of writing that students complete during the term for their language arts grade. If writing is your focus, you might extend your writers workshops into new genres and topics by pulling information from content area topics. The content area classes can be used to help students gather information for their writing. Writers workshop can be used for both writing and writing instruction. Use the suggestions in this book to complement the work that you are already doing in writers workshop.

When you start to contemplate integrating writing across the curriculum, scheduling is one area that demands great attention. The chart on page 9 gives a six-week sample schedule for unit plans for content area classes and language arts classes. It shows how writing and concept instruction can be integrated. In this example, the teacher teaches language arts, mathematics, social studies, science, health, and art. Students have time for writing throughout the content area unit of study and during writers workshop time in language arts. The chart on page 10 gives a six-week sample schedule for writing in content area units only.

Leonora, a grade-8 science teacher, does not include a written project for every science unit. She usually selects a few science units each year that provide plenty of scope for students' writing. Students carry out writing projects during these units, but, during the rest of the year, students' writing in science includes the more traditional note-taking and short-answer writing. Leonora does, however, emphasize elements of good writing in her feedback and assessments of all the writing that students do in her science classes. By doing this, she demonstrates that all teachers are writing teachers and that communicating effectively through writing is important in all subject areas, not just language arts.

SCHEDULE FOR TEACHERS WHO TEACH LANGUAGE ARTS AND CONTENT AREA CLASSES

	Content Classes	Language Arts Classes
Week One	• Students and teacher complete a K-W-L for the content topic. • Students read about the unit topic, discuss the topic in small groups. • Students do hands-on activities related to the content-area topic. • The teacher introduces the writing assignment and shows examples of the genres that students could choose to use in their writing.	• Students continue with free-choice writing that they have been doing in writers workshop.
Weeks Two through Five	• Students continue reading about the topic. • Students continue doing hands-on activities related to the content area topic. • The teacher devotes four or five 40-minute content area classes to the writing assignment. • The teacher continues to conference with students and teaches mini-lessons to support students' writing.	• Students continue with their free-choice writing. • Students begin planning and gathering information and writing for the content-area writing assignment. • The teacher writes along with the students and teaches mini-lessons on the assigned genre for the content area writing assignment.
Week Six	• Students continue to write, revise, and edit their writing. • Students complete their writing and read it to a partner in a small group or to the whole class. • The end product or published writing may be sent out to a more public audience. • The teacher celebrates and assesses the writing.	• Students use some writers workshop time for content area writing and their free-choice writing. • The teacher continues to conference with students. • The teacher continues teaching mini-lessons to support students' writing for content area and other writing.

TOPICS AND TIME

In writers workshop, to get students to say something worthwhile in their writing, teachers usually open topic and genre possibilities to whatever students can imagine. Sometimes, however, you might assign topics and genres; students will find it easier to venture into new territory and try something that they would not try on their own if you left their choices totally open. The same is true in content area writing. The difference is that we provide students with a range of topics that are related to the content area learning objectives. These

SCHEDULE FOR TEACHERS WHO TEACH CONTENT AREA CLASSES ONLY

Weeks One and Two

- Students read about the unit topic, discuss the topic in small groups, and do hands-on activities related to the content-area topic as they would in any content area unit.
- The teacher introduces the writing assignment and shows how content area topics can be incorporated into many genres.
- Students begin planning, gathering information through reading, and doing hands-on activities.
- Students write a first draft.

In some classes, 15 to 20 minutes are devoted to writing. In other classes, all of the time is used for reading, discussing, and hands-on activities.

Weeks Three Through Five

- Students continue reading about the topic and doing hands-on activities related to the content area topic.
- Students continue planning, gathering information, and drafting their writing.
- The teacher continues to teach mini-lessons to support students' writing.

In some classes, 15 to 20 minutes are devoted to writing, conferencing, and so on. In others, 20 to 40 minutes are devoted to writing and writing instruction. There may be a few classes devoted entirely to reading and hands-on activities. During this time, students think about how the reading and activities can contribute to their writing. They may be doing some writing at home as well.

Week Six

- Students continue to write, revise, and edit their writing.
- Students complete their writing and read it to a partner in small groups or to the whole class.
- Students may send their end product or published writing out to a more public audience.
- The teacher celebrates and assesses the writing.

Leslie is a grade-6 science teacher. She asked her students to show what they had learned about levers and motion. They wrote using their choice of genre and came up with some creative and fulfilling products. Because she planned to use the students' writing in her assessment for a unit on motion, Leslie asked her students to ensure that they include in their writing at least two of nine concepts (e.g., motion, oscillation, linear motion, rotational motion, reciprocating motion, force, friction, fulcrum, and lever). Beyond that, Leslie's students had full control of the topics and genres they used in their writing. At other times, the parameters for writing in the content areas may be placed on the genre. This forces students to stretch beyond those genres that they gravitate toward and are most comfortable with. Encouraging students to stretch beyond their comfort level can foster greater creativity.

allow students to extend and enrich their conceptual learning and also to demonstrate their learning through writing. I do, however, caution against assigning a very narrow topic (for example, the life cycle of a mealworm) or dictating an opening sentence that all students must use (e.g., Would you believe that your body size and shape are influenced by diet, exercise, and the size and shape of your parents and grandparents?). If we want their writing to be a tool for discovery and new learning, we should always give students some choice. It will then be more worthwhile, it will say something, and it will be meaningful for the student.

Regardless of how narrowly defined the topic or genre for the writing might be, students need to be well informed about the topic, and they need some experience with the genre. No one can write from inside a vacuum. The types of activities that have long been associated with teaching in content area classes—working with concrete materials, going on field trips, doing interviews, reading print-based materials of all types, and having small-group discussions, for example—provide the information. This means that the format of content area classes does not have to change drastically when you are integrating writing. You may need to help your students determine the types of information that will be important and help them record that information so it can be used later in their writing. These skills, together with helping students organize the information, will be the topics of mini-lessons presented in later chapters. In chapter 3, I present numerous suggestions for supporting students in searching for, recording, and organizing information for their writing.

When you are incorporating writing into content area classes, you will be faced with the challenge of allotting adequate time to support students in their writing. This includes time to complete mini-lessons on writing, time devoted to writing, and time for conferencing with the students about what they have written. If you are both a content area teacher and a language arts teacher, you can borrow time from writers workshop in language arts periods. If you are exclusively a content area teacher, you will need to take some time from other activities and devote it to writing. There will not likely be enough time in class for students to do all their writing, so they will have to do some writing at home on their own time.

Students who have put a great deal of effort and time into their writing will want it to be read by a wider audience than just their teacher. Indeed, their motivation for and commitment to writing will be much higher if they know that their writing will have an effect on someone else and will not simply be the source of a grade on their report card. It is important that you plan opportunities for students to share their writing with others. The audience can be a small group of peers, the whole class, students in another class or school, or readers of a local newspaper. In one of my classes, for example, students created handbooks on caring for animals. Their handbooks were distributed to local veterinarian offices and became reading material for pet owners as they waited to have their pets attended to.

CLASSROOM ORGANIZATIONAL ISSUES

My experience with grades 4 to 8 students shows that they find the idea of writing in science, social studies, health, or any other subject area very appealing. Students get excited at the thought of using stories, cartoons, letters, and so on to demonstrate their learning and to learn more about the topics. The challenge for their teacher is to organize the class so that students' interests are sustained and their writing is supported.

Donald Graves (1994) tells us that, "if children are to choose topics or figure out how they will solve writing problems, they need a highly predictable classroom" (p. 111). For example:

1. Students should write regularly.

2. Students should start each class by taking out their folders, notebooks, or binders and reviewing what they have written up to that point. They might use these notebooks, folders, or binders to store the information they gather and to organize drafts of their writing. Because students may be collecting artifacts, newspaper clippings, and printouts from websites, folders or binders might be more practical than notebooks. I borrow from

Khaled is a grade-5 social studies teacher. He assigned a persuasive letter on an issue that had arisen in a unit on First Nation peoples of North America. He wanted to introduce students to a type of writing that they rarely chose in their free-choice writing. In this case, the genre was determined by the teacher, but his students had a wide range of topics within the content area from which to choose. All these topics satisfied the learning outcomes.

Leonora, a grade-8 science teacher, found that her students enjoyed doing much of their writing at home. They often got feedback from their peers by emailing their emerging drafts to their peers or by reading over the phone what they had written. This kind of individual effort to communicate their writing was a welcome result of incorporating writing into the content area.

Camille Allen's (2001) suggestions to help students organize their notebooks, folders, or binders. I have my students divide them into two sections: (1) Portfolio and (2) Resources. Students keep drafts of their writing in the Portfolio section and keep the computer printouts, the notes they have taken while reading, viewing, or interviewing, or from any other sources of information they are planning to use for their writing, in the Resources section.

3. Students should be aware of routines for:
   - getting supplies
   - signalling to the teacher for help
   - gathering information from books and magazines in the classroom or school library, or from the classroom or computer-lab computers
   - scheduling a student-teacher conference with the teacher
   - determining how they will read their writing to a peer audience

4. Students sharing drafts of their writing in small groups works well if there are many students who want to share at the same time. If one student wants to read a very long piece, he/she might be given a time limit and instructions to summarize some parts and then read other parts to stay within the time limit.

5. Teacher and students need to negotiate acceptable noise levels and allocate time for quiet writing, for student-teacher conferences, and for reading published writing to the class.

6. When students have finished a piece, they can start another one, or they can read or do hands-on projects, computer work, or any other work that will give them information or inspiration for writing another piece. They might also create multimedia presentations of their writing.

7. Try to set up the structures of process-writing classrooms (Calkins 1994; Graves 1994), which provides the predictability that students need. These structures allow for students to work with peers, either formally in author groups or less formally in peer conferences. When assigning due dates for drafts and final products, and when planning mini-lessons, take care to respect students' unique writing processes rather than expect all students to plan one day, draft the next day, revise the following day, and then edit the final day before handing in an assignment.

8. Your role as teacher is to serve as a model by writing alongside the students. You also need to provide ongoing feedback on students' writing, either in formal student-teacher conferences or in informal conversations while students are writing.

Author Groups

Students could meet formally with peers (two to four students per group) to provide feedback about each others' writing. In these groups, students and teacher (when it is appropriate) read drafts of their own writing. Group members take turns describing what is effective and also explain what is unclear, confusing, or needs to be revised. The goal is to build students' confidence as writers and to give them a sense of the impression that their writing is making on their audience. You may need to show students how to provide constructive suggestions to other writers. Students often feel vulnerable when reading their written work to peers, so it is important that you establish expectations and model respectful ways to make suggestions within the groups.

Peer Conferences

If you set up classrooms so that students can talk to one another while they write, they can share their ideas with peers and use these ideas in their writing. They can also receive ongoing feedback about how clearly they communicate their ideas and about how their peers will accept their writing.

Feedback to Students

After teaching a mini-lesson, you might schedule student-teacher conferences or walk around the classroom responding to students' requests for assistance and reading students' writing as they compose. I usually schedule no more than one or two conferences in any 40-minute period and keep each of them to five or ten minutes. During these teacher-student conversations, I usually ask students what they want feedback on and then also comment on aspects of the writing that strike me as strong or as needing revision or editing. Sometimes I concentrate on specific aspects that have been addressed in mini-lessons. In chapter 9 (see pp. 67–70), I provide further suggestions for giving feedback to students.

Writing Alongside Students

Teachers can show the value of writing by sharing their own joys and challenges as they write alongside their students. Students will see that, even though adults (their teachers, for instance), sometimes get frustrated with the writing process, they still see writing as important and rewarding. Often, in the first 10 minutes of a writing class, I write at the overhead projector or SmartBoard so that students can see the way my writing is evolving; I can monitor what my students are doing at the same time.

Students' Personal Writing Processes

Any writing model is a presentation of some writers' writing processes rather than a universal writing process. Often, writers engage in some form of planning and thinking through of ideas prior to writing, either in their heads or on paper, through brainstorming, or by sketching or listing. Before publication, they do some initial drafts, then revise their writing, and finally do some editing. The process does not look the same for every writer, nor does it occur in the same order for every writer. We must respect the idiosyncratic nature of writing and be open to all students' specific needs for help with the planning, drafting, revising, and editing stages as they work toward a satisfying written product.

WORKS CITED

Allen, C. *The Multigenre Research Paper: Voice, Passion, and Discovery in Grades 4–6*. Portsmouth, NH: Heinemann, 2001.

Calkins, L. *The Art of Teaching Writing*, 2nd ed. Portsmouth, NH: Heinemann, 1994.

Graves, D. *A Fresh Look at Writing*. Portsmouth, NH: Heinemann, 1994.

> *Today's students live in a world where increases in the amount of information being produced will continue to be exponential. They need to be savvy users of information. They need to know how information works and how information can work for them.*
>
> —Carol Koechlin and Sandi Zwaan

Seeking, Recording, and Organizing Information

Chapter 3

THE INFORMATION SEARCH

The words of Carol Koechlin and Sandi Zwaan (above) express what we all recognize—that an ever-expanding universe of information is available to our students. Our challenge is to nurture students' curiosity about the world and help them access the information in order to answer questions, solve problems, and imagine what could be.

For some students, accessing information from a variety of sources will be second nature. Others will need support using the Internet or their school or public libraries. Some may also need help finding appropriate books, articles, pamphlets, videos, and posters at the appropriate reading levels. We cannot assume that students know how to use the library's filing system. Furthermore, once students have books in their hands, we cannot assume that they know how to use the table of contents and the index to locate information. We need to seek out every opportunity to teach and reinforce these skills.

Part I: Mini-Lessons for Seeking Information on the Internet

The Internet is an enormous and sometimes overwhelming resource for students seeking ideas and information for their content writing. Although a number of search engines are available, the one that most students and teachers use is Google <www.google.ca>. This website has developed its own language and has become a verb: "Why don't you try 'googling' that to find out more?" If students are looking for an alternative, they might try <www.hotbot.com>. Hotbot allows students to conduct advanced searches with a filter for finding keywords in any position on a web page (e.g., in the title, in the URL, or in the body of the text). It allows students to filter their search by date. From Hotbot, students can also access Google and Ask Jeeves, which is a search engine that acts on specific questions.

Leonora, a grade-8 science teacher, reinforces information-searching skills every time she asks students to find a page in their science textbooks. Instead of directing them to a particular page, she gives students the topic and asks them to use the table of contents, the index, or headings and subheadings of chapters to find the correct page. She also supports them in shaping questions that will focus their information searches. Students need help to identify relevant information, make connections among ideas, and organize the information into meaningful themes.

Two skills are particularly important for locating reliable information on the Internet and from other print and visual media sources: (1) using keywords, and (2) assessing the credibility of sources of information.

Mini-Lesson I.1: Keyword Searches

Demonstrations and guided practice are the best ways to support students in narrowing down terms for searching on the Internet or in other sources. Walk your students through a search using a topic addressed in your content area. See the chart below for information and tips for narrowing a keyword search. Follow up with guided practice in a whole-class or small-group lesson, as you help students narrow their focus to useful keywords for topics addressed in the unit of study. This guided practice leads to independent practice. Have students conduct keyword searches on their own for the topics they have selected for their writing.

Mini-Lesson I.2: Assessing Quality of Information

Students need to recognize that not all the information on the Internet can be trusted, nor is it necessarily accurate. Anyone can put information on a website, regardless of her/his motivation, credentials, depth of knowledge, or skill level.

NARROWING A KEYWORD SEARCH

Topic

What do properties of air and principles of flight have to do with being able to fly in an airplane? A search using these key words will yield the following hits:

properties air – 13 500 000 hits

properties air flight – 1 470 000 hits

properties-of-air airplane – 6 770 hits

properties of air, principles of flight – 177 hits

In the final keyword search, the number of hits (177) is still high, but the descriptions of the websites show that the majority will provide useful information to answer the research question. Internet search engines list the sites from highest to lowest probability that you will find what you are looking for at the topic, given the search words you typed in. Generally, students will find something relevant in the first two pages of the list on any search engine and can avoid wild-goose chases.

Tips for Searches

1. Search engines ignore common words and characters such as *where* and *how*, as well as certain single digits and single letters, because they tend to slow down a search without improving the results. It is not necessary to include *and* in the search, because the search engine assumes you want both terms included, not just one of them.

2. If a common word is essential to getting the results you want, you can include it by putting a space and a plus sign (+) in front of it.

3. If you want to narrow the search to the most specific topic, use quotation marks around the phrase. The search engine will look for only the exact words in the exact order you have typed them.

The intention and the perspective of the creators should also be considered in books and other media, including the Internet. Encourage students to determine the creator's or designer's purpose for creating print or visual media. Students should assess the diversity of viewpoints presented and how thoroughly and thoughtfully the writers and producers have explained each perspective. They might not be aware that the presence or absence of particular information may be deliberate. Attention or inattention to perspectives and unconscious assumptions about the topic can sometimes lead a writer in narrow directions. In addition to fostering students' awareness of the creator's underlying assumptions, you might also need to help students recognize stereotypes that present unwarranted biases toward certain groups of people and values. Assessing the quality of information also includes determining the depth of knowledge that authors and designers bring to their writing and visual creations. Students should look at the number of sources consulted by the creator and determine how recently the information was reported. Population numbers or information about scientific discoveries quickly become outdated, for example. As a general rule, it is best for students to read a number of sources on a topic, not just one. Students can then compare and contrast the information of various sources and determine which facts and ideas appear most frequently. They should also look up information on the sources of the information to determine the contributor's level of expertise. More experienced researchers can look at the references that the creators consult in their own information gathering. This will show how widely they sought out their information and help determine how trusted their information can be. In teaching students to judge the quality of sources, you may demonstrate strategies for using Internet, print, and visual media on topics of study in content area classes. Students may find the questions listed in BLM 3.1 helpful when they are searching for information.

Mini-Lesson I.3: Developing Questions for Interviews

The interview, a helpful tool for gathering information from people, is an excellent alternative to accessing information in print, electronic, or visual form. Developing interview questions is difficult for students of all ages. Students need to understand what information they are seeking before they can define how to best develop their questions. The questions need to be created in such a way as to help the interviewee focus her/his response on the desired topic. One of the more difficult concepts for students to understand is the difference between open-ended and closed questions.

In this mini-lesson, students explore how to make their questions clear so that the interviewee knows what kind of information to provide. They also explore how to ask questions that give interviewees some room to respond (see BLM 3.2). After they have done this mini-lesson, students could draw up a list of considerations for developing interview questions and create their own interview questions.

Part II: Mini-Lessons for Recording Information

Mini-Lesson II.1: Selecting Relevant Information

In an effort not to overlook important details when taking notes, students often write down more information than they need. The end result is a page of notes that looks similar to the original source. For most students, developing the skill of selecting only relevant information will likely require a great deal of modelling and guided support. Encourage students to think about the following questions as they read a book, magazine, pamphlet, or website about their topic:

- What kinds of information do you expect to find as you read the headings?
- What information directly answers your questions?
- What information is interesting but doesn't really answer your questions?

Introduce students to different ways of thinking by demonstrating what information is relevant when taking notes from a source. Use BLM 3.3 as a sample demonstration. In this example, the student has highlighted the parts of the text that are useful in answering a specific question about glaciers and has explained why she thinks this information is relevant.

Mini-Lesson II.2: Three Forms of Note Taking

1. Using sentence stems: Maureen Lewis, David Wray, and Patricia Rospigliosi (1994) propose using sentence stems to help students write notes in their own words. I modified their work by adding sentence stems that help students focus on what they are learning as they read, view, observe, or experience new ideas and information.

   Have students use the template in BLM 3.4 or ask them to write the stems that work best for their notes. The sample shown in BLM 3.5 demonstrates how students can use the template. Note that this example is not complete; the student still has additional information to locate and some discrepant information to verify.

2. Notes and thoughts: Writing down notes and thoughts is valuable because it encourages students to think deeply about information as they take notes. It is both a note-taking form and a forum for exploratory writing. In this form, students take notes in point form and then reflect on what the information means to them. They draw on previous experiences and background knowledge and may bring in other information by asking a peer or their teacher. This form provides space for wondering, hypothesizing, and planning what students might try in the future. See BLM 3.6, which contains a helpful template for students to use. Also see BLM 3.7, which contains a good example of one student's use of the notes-and-thoughts format.

3. The Cornell note-taking framework: In the Cornell note-taking framework, students make connections between their questions and the information they find about the topic. Encourage students to make connections and reflect on what the notes mean to them. This summary and analysis allows for some exploratory thinking about the topic. Give your students a copy of the Cornell

note-taking framework (BLM 3.8), which is based on the work of Walter Pauk (1974). You might make an overhead transparency of BLM 3.9 and have a discussion of how one student used the framework to take notes from Linda Granfield's *Where Poppies Grow.*

Part III: Mini-Lessons for Organizing Information

Mini-Lesson III.1: K-W-L

Donna Ogle (1986) introduced teachers to K-W-L, a structure for gathering information, which has become ubiquitous in classrooms. Students assess what they know (K) about a topic, ask questions about what (W) they want to learn, and then read/view/observe/survey/interview to learn (L) more about that topic. This structure helps students think about specific types of information that they should search for in preparation for their writing. The questions help students organize the information they gather. The information can be made into headings and subheadings for students' writing. BLM 3.10 is a template that can be used by students to organize their information in a K-W-L format.

Mini-Lesson III.2: Using Compare/Contrast Charts

A compare/contrast format for taking notes helps students organize information when a writing task requires them to compare and contrast two ideas, people, or things. (See template in BLM 3.11; see also BLM 3.12, which gives an example of how a pair of students took notes about the differences and similarities between the two key figures in Canadian Confederation.) See BLM 5.8 for a poem that the students wrote about the two historic figures. Have your students identify how the students in BLM 3.12 used the notes to construct the two voices in the poem in BLM 5.8.

Mini-Lesson III.3: Developing Outlines

Outlines give students a global sense of the information they have gathered and make clear the connections among the ideas. A good outline gives students a clearer idea of where they will be moving with their writing. Without an outline, students may become confused and may try to include too little or too much information in their writing. In the writing process, however, students should not be expected to follow their outlines to the letter. New ideas arise as students write and gather information, and new directions emerge for their writing. Encourage students to stray from the outline to some extent to allow for deeper understandings. We would be disappointed if students' thinking was the same at the end of their writing as it had been when they created their outlines. The process of developing an outline is helpful for many students, but it should not be a requirement if they have developed other ways to organize their ideas.

During this mini-lesson, have students begin by reading the sample notes and thoughts (see BLM 3.13) and circling the ideas that fit together. They might cut them out and paste them together physically or on the computer (see BLM 3.14) for one way to organize them into an outline. Once they have placed the similar ideas together, have students think about what all the related ideas are saying and come up with the big ideas (or themes). Then have them write the emerging themes as headings for each category. It is not necessary to prepare formal outlines using numbering systems. The students who created BLM 3.14 organized their notes and found connections among the examples and the supporting details. They clustered them together under the appropriate descriptive headings. From their outline with the headings and supporting information, students can now readily begin to write about Alexander Graham Bell.

WORKS CITED

Koechlin, C., and S. Zwaan. *Info Tasks for Successful Learning: Building Skills in Reading, Writing, and Research.* Markham, ON: Pembroke, 2001.

Lewis, M., D. Wray, and P. Rospigliosi. "And I Want It in Your Own Words." *The Reading Teacher* 47.7 (1994), 528–536.

Ogle, D. "K-W-L: A Teaching Model that Develops Active Reading of Expository Text." *The Reading Teacher* 39 (1986), 563–570.

Pauk, W. *How to Study in College.* Boston, MA: Houghton Mifflin, 1974.

Writing Non-Narrative Across the Curriculum

Chapter **4**

WHY WRITE NON-NARRATIVE IN CONTENT AREAS?

When we speak of teaching writing, we are usually referring to narrative writing. I use the term *non-narrative* instead of *nonfiction* because I am focusing on the form rather than on whether the content is factual or imagined. In most cases, narrative writing seems to overshadow other types of writing in elementary classrooms. You will likely find more narrative than non-narrative writing in students' portfolios and on display in school hallways. Lists of teaching resources are composed mainly of narrative writing rather than non-narrative writing. Narrative seems to be viewed as the genre of greater choice—like a fine box of chocolates. Non-narrative seems to be viewed as the genre of necessity—like a sack of potatoes.

Yet, the "chocolate side" of non-narrative is evident to writers like Aldous Huxley. In the quote that opens this chapter, he sees enormous scope in writing using the non-narrative essay. According to Huxley, students can write about any topic of their choice, saying whatever is important to them using non-narrative forms. Students have a multitude of choices in determining which form might best suit their intended purpose (see chart on p. 23). The broad range of topics and forms makes non-narrative a type of writing that is "most likely to spur children's passion and wonder for learning" (Harvey 2002, p. 12). I have observed students glued to the Internet or to magazines, willing to invest time and energy outside of class in their desire to learn more about a topic and to communicate that learning using non-narrative genres. Many reluctant readers and writers, both boys and girls, choose non-narrative in their reading and writing outside of school (Booth 2002).

In spite of the wide range of opportunities for communicating information and many students' obvious interest in non-narrative, researchers like Suzanne Hidi and Angela Hildyard (1983) found that adolescents have less control of non-narrative forms of writing than they do of narrative forms. They questioned whether non-narrative is inherently more difficult to write or whether students had less experience in writing non-narrative in the early grades of their schooling. My hunch is that the latter is true. There is ample evidence that non-narrative writing is as natural as narrative writing. Marie Clay (1975) found that spontaneous writing by five-year-old children took the form of lists of the letters, numbers, and words that they knew. We know that preschool children can communicate ideas in non-narrative form when they talk. Among the many ways they use language, young children ask questions, tell us about things they have seen, and give directions about what they want us to do. More and more often, researchers are finding that narrative is not the only way that young children represent their worlds (Kamberelis 1999). In this

IDEAS FOR WRITING NON-NARRATIVE ACROSS THE CURRICULUM

Social Studies
Have students:

- write a diary or blog of someone who lived during a period of time covered in the curriculum

- write a persuasive essay on a controversial current issue

Science
Have students:

- write a script for an interview with certain organisms (or a television show like "This Is Your Life"), showing their life cycles

- design an advertisement for a model solar heating device designed and constructed by students

Mathematics
Have students:

- write an explanation for carrying out a particular operation

- design and conduct a survey, and record the results on a labelled graph or table

Art
Have students:

- design a poster with both a visual design and text with student-created fonts to advertise a sculpture that students have created

- write a review of a favourite artist's work, using students' understanding of line, shape, form, texture, and colour

Health
Have students:

- write an advice column on interpersonal relationships or healthy eating topics in the curriculum

- write instructions on how to give basic first aid

Music
Have students:

- create a glossary of music terms that they have learned

- create a PowerPoint presentation that describes and contains excerpts of music from a particular historical era (e.g., Renaissance, Baroque, Classical, Romantic) chapter, I present suggestions for non-narrative writing across the curriculum. In addition to lists of non-narrative forms that students might choose in their writing, I present ideas for helping students recognize what particular non-narrative forms can help them achieve.

NON-NARRATIVE FORMS

We write to achieve particular purposes. We write to come to know ourselves and answer questions about our world. We hope to build relationships with our readers and hope that readers enjoy our writing. We tend to use non-narrative forms for three reasons: to persuade, to inform or explain, and to instruct or direct (Halliday 1975).

Often, a particular non-narrative form may serve more than one purpose, so classifying the forms according to purpose is difficult. The chart below shows some forms of writing that appear in different categories and that serve more than one purpose. The other forms of writing are categorized according to their primary functions.

NON-NARRATIVE FORMS: A SHORT LIST

Forms that Persuade	Forms that Inform or Explain	Forms that Instruct or Direct
book reviews	book reviews	directions
advertisements	summaries	web pages
web pages	reports	instructions
persuasive essays	web pages	explanations
PowerPoint presentations	memos	PowerPoint presentations
blogs	interview scripts	advice columns
written debates	documentaries (video or audio)	blogs
commentaries	case studies	recipes
cditorials	PowerPoint presentations	manuals
advice columns	monographs	procedures
letters	radio or television newscasts	posters
posters	letters	rules
want ads	newspaper articles	

HELPING STUDENTS BECOME BETTER NON-NARRATIVE WRITERS AND LEARN CONTENT KNOWLEDGE

Part I: Mini-Lessons for Getting to Know the Possibilities and Demands of Genres

Mini-Lesson I.1: Introducing a Variety of Genres

The best way I have found for introducing non-narrative writing is to have students read various genres. Students will come to see that any number of genres can be used to communicate the information in their content area subjects. (See appendix C for a list of books, organized by subject area and annotated according to form, that you might use as a guide.) The challenge for students is to learn how each genre is structured to accomplish particular purposes. We do not want students to see genres as rigid sets of organizational structures. Instead, we want to show students that the structures of non-narrative genres are ever-evolving. They change to fit the contexts in which they are used. The most important thing about non-narrative genres is that writers can use them for their own purposes. I recommend finding as many examples as possible of particular genres for students to read, pointing out the similarities and differences in how the writers have adapted the non-narrative genre structures for their own purposes. When you read to students, you might ask questions such as those listed in the chart below.

After thinking about the structure of the genre and the ways in which writers can use the genre to communicate information, students will have a starting point for their own writing. The next three activities are designed to narrow students' focus on features of three types of non-narrative writing.

Mini-Lesson I.2: Identifying Features of Non-Narrative Writing that Is Meant to Inform

The list of non-narrative forms that provide information is lengthy. Generally, when we think of non-narrative forms, we think of those that inform (e.g., reports, summaries, documentaries, memos, newspaper articles, catalogues, radio or television news reports, websites). Our students read and listen to these and other non-narrative texts daily. Many students internalize features of

---

QUESTIONS FOR CONSIDERING WHAT VARIOUS GENRES HAVE TO OFFER AND WHAT FORMATS THEY USE

1. What did you learn about _____ (topic)?

2. Show the paragraphs, sentences, lines, or words that give information about the topic.

3. How did the writer communicate the information in this type of text (genre)?

4. What makes this genre different from a story? From a poem?

5. How is this example of a _____ (whatever the genre is) similar to and different from this other example?

6. What advice would you give to someone who is about to write using this genre?

texts that inform and can readily use these genres in their content area writing. Other students need support in recognizing them. In this mini-lesson, ask your students to compare and contrast two types of writing that inform: a student-composed newspaper article (see BLM 4.1) and a student-written report (see BLM 4.2). Both deal with the same topic: simple machines. Students can use the chart in BLM 4.3 to guide their analysis of the two non-narrative texts.

Students will likely note that non-narrative text intended to inform tends to have a main idea/detail structure. The writer states or implies the key ideas that she/he is trying to convey and then provides specific, detailed information to elaborate on the main ideas. Headings and subheadings are often used, depending on the type of non-narrative text, to help readers identify the key ideas. The title is usually descriptive and conveys the text's overall idea. Students can use the information gathered from reading either the two student-written texts reproduced in BLM 4.1 and BLM 4.2, or others from their lives, to write non-narrative texts that inform readers about the topic in your content area.

Mini-Lesson I.3: Identifying Features of Non-Narrative Writing that Is Meant to Persuade

Young people often present an opinion with more than adequate emotional investment about some topics. For example, some students may argue that they should be allowed to go to a friend's party; otherwise, their lives will be ruined or the world as they know it will end. Writing persuasively about topics in various content areas requires more than emotional investment, however; students need a wider repertoire of tools than just their emotional response for content area persuasive writing.

Reading and analyzing examples of persuasive writing (e.g., letters to the editor, editorials, advice columns, blogs, advertisements, commentaries, book reviews) help to develop in students a sense of what they can achieve by writing non-narrative texts. The student writing samples in BLM 4.4 (a blog on a mathematics topic) and BLM 4.5 (a persuasive essay on an art topic) are useful for demonstrating persuasive writing possibilities. Students might comment on what they have learned from the two persuasive pieces and what further information they would like writers to include. They might also discuss the level of interest that the writers have generated in their writing and how they have made their writing interesting. Students completing the chart in BLM 4.6 will likely notice the following characteristics of persuasive writing:

- The writer states her/his position somewhere in the introduction (perhaps in the title) and again at the end.

- The writer states at least one reason showing that she/he has taken this position.

- The writer provides at least one reason showing that others might oppose his/her position and refutes the reason(s).

When students write their own persuasive papers on topics that relate to their daily lives, they can draw on their analysis of the two samples and of other persuasive writing.

Mini-Lesson I.4: Identifying Features of Non-Narrative Writing that Is Meant to Instruct or Direct

Young people have been instructing others about what they want and trying to direct others to get what they want from a very early age. Even before babies can talk, they use gestures, sounds, and facial expressions to direct their caregivers to feed them or bring them a toy, for example. As students go through school, their need to instruct or direct others does not diminish, but the topics for the instructions and directions become more complex. In this mini-lesson, have students compare and contrast two types of writing that instruct and direct. BLM 4.7 explains a healthy lifestyle and BLM 4.8 gives a "recipe" for healthy living. Have students use the chart in BLM 4.9 to guide their analysis of the two non-narrative texts. Students will likely note that instructive or directive texts tend to present information in steps or lists and use specific verbs that have the implied *you* as their subject. Have students comment on what they have learned from the two texts and what further information they would like writers to include. Also have them discuss the level of interest that the writers have generated in their writing and how they have made their writing interesting. When students write their own texts designed to instruct or direct, they can draw on their analysis of the two samples and of other writing found in their daily lives.

Part II: Mini-Lessons for Teaching Content and Organization

Mini-Lesson II.1: Maintaining a Focus

In this mini-lesson on maintaining focus, have students read a first draft and a final draft (BLM 4.10) of one student's report on soil erosion. Ask them to determine how well each draft stays on topic and what the writer did to make the second draft more focused. Use the following questions to help students identify the focus in the two drafts:

- Which title gives you more information about the topic of the essay?

- What information do you get from the introductory paragraphs of each version? Which introductory paragraph stays on the same topic throughout the piece?

- What are the key ideas of each paragraph in the two essays? Which paragraphs are easiest to follow—the ones with a single key idea or the ones with many different ideas?

- How does the writer connect each paragraph to the one before it? (What phrases or words does she/he use?)

- Compare and contrast the two versions of the essay. What recommendations can you make to writers about staying on one topic?

Mini-Lesson II.2: Supporting the Main Point with Examples and Details

In this mini-lesson, have students assess how well the writer has supported his main ideas with examples and details presented in BLM 4.11. Then have them use the writer's notes in the compare/contrast chart in BLM 4.12 to determine what revisions he might make to provide stronger support for his position. Use the following questions to help students focus their attention on the writer's use of supporting details:

- What is the writer's main point?
- What details and examples provide information about the main point?
- What other information could the writer have included in the report?
- Where could the writer have included this information?

Have students work in pairs or as a whole class to revise the report, adding the information from the writer's notes on the compare/contrast chart and other information they find in books, in magazines, or on the Internet.

Mini-Lesson II.3: Including Quotes from References

For the most part, we want non-narrative writing to be in the students' own words. We encourage this for the simple reason that word-for-word copying from other sources does not foster deep thinking about a topic. We need to explain the term *plagiarism* to students and in our teaching caution against it. Sometimes, however, quotes are needed and can add interest to the student's writing. Explaining how and when to use quotes is often difficult, and students have some trouble deciding what is appropriate and what is not.

There are two main questions that need to be answered: (1) How much of the quote should be used, especially if the original text is very long? (2) How many quotes can be included so as not to overwhelm the student's own writing? These questions can be very difficult for students in any grade level. When many long passages are included in a paper, it becomes difficult to figure out what our student writers are thinking. When quotes dominate a paper, there is no coherent flow of the student's thought. Frequent quotes scattered throughout a paper can chop up the writing and make it hard to follow. When used properly, quotes should support the writer's argument and add clarity to thoughts.

BLM 4.13 provides tips to help students decide when and how to use quotes. These are not hard-and-fast rules but are designed to help students avoid typical problems. BLM 4.14 shows a good example of one student's use of quotes.

Mini-Lesson II.4: Audience Awareness–
Using Elements of Graphic Design

We all know that the manner in which material is presented is important to our interest in and understanding of that material. A writer's awareness of audience perceptions and motivations is key to communicating important messages. Regardless of whether writers use computers or their own handwriting, they should pay attention to the arrangement of the text and graphics on their page. Today's students are more conscious than ever of the role that graphic design plays in their lives. They often include elements of design in their written assignments automatically, without being asked to do so.

Graphic design includes both page layout and typography (Moline 1995). Page layout is the positioning of all the visual elements of the work, including the printed text. Laying out a page means paying attention to the arrangement of text into paragraphs or columns, and how headings, borders, arrows, lines, bullets, and so on, are used. The process of laying out a page helps writers organize information, make connections between text and graphics, and highlight certain important information. Typography includes more than just the typeface but also the size of font and its style, whether bold, italicized, or underlined. BLM 4.15 identifies some layout and typography features that students can consider when designing the final drafts of their content area writing. To add to students' awareness of elements of graphic design, ask them to assess the effectiveness of lines and white space, fonts, and headings and subheadings in print and online non-narrative texts.

WORKS CITED

Booth, D. *Even Hockey Players Read: Boys, Literacy and Learning*. Markham, ON: Pembroke, 2002.

Clay, M. *What Did I Write?* Portsmouth, NH: Heinemann, 1975.

Halliday, M. A. K. *Learning How to Mean*. New York: Elsevier North-Holland, Inc., 1975.

Harvey, S., "Nonfiction Inquiry: Using Real Reading and Writing to Explore the World." *Language Arts* 80.1 (2002), 12–22.

Hidi, S., and A. Hildyard. "The Comparison of Oral and Written Productions in Two Discourse Types." *Discourse Processes* 91 (1983), 91–105.

Kamberelis, G. "Genre Development and Learning: Children Writing Stories, Science Reports, and Poems." *Research in the Teaching of English* 33 (1999), 403–460.

Moline, S. *I See What You Mean: Children at Work with Visual Information*. Markham, ON: Pembroke, 1995.

Robertson, C. (ed.) *The Dictionary of Quotations*. Hertfordshire, UK: Wordsworthy Editions, 1997.

Poems hang out where life is.

—Susan Goldsmith Wooldridge

Writing Poetry Across the Curriculum

Chapter 5

WHY WRITE POETRY IN CONTENT AREAS?

Poetry probably does not leap to mind when you think of writing possibilities within content areas. Yet, Susan Goldsmith Wooldridge (above) places poetry squarely in the middle of everyday life, which is where most topics in science, social studies, music, art, mathematics, and health are also found. Poetry has untapped potential for communication and discovery in all subject areas, because it is hidden in so many of the things we encounter in everyday life. Paul Corrigan (2002) says that students "need to see the concrete, work-a-day manner in which poetry is and can be woven into their existence" (p. 33). Content area classes provide many opportunities for concrete, hands-on experiences. In this chapter, I provide suggestions for using poetry to capture the learning that comes from these kinds of experiences.

Poetry provides a vibrant forum for thinking, as it allows students to distill experience using just a few words. David Booth and Bill Moore (2003) say, "The more we mess about with words, the more intrigued with words do we become. The more words we have at our disposal, the better we can think, thus the better we can write" (p. 106). At the same time that students are playing with words to create a poem, they are also playing with ideas, and this is a great place for learning to happen. When writing poetry, students are like scientists. They become attentive to the sensory information in their world and to the clues in the texts they read (Cullinan, Scala, and Schroder 1995). As they trim away extraneous words and replace vague words with more precise ones, students are refining and sharpening their understanding of the ideas.

Some teachers keep poetry writing on the margins because it seems difficult and inaccessible. These apprehensions are fairly widespread. I recently read about a study that Ellen Strenski and Nancy Giller Esposito conducted in 1980. When they asked their college students to define poetry, the students focused on rhythm, rhyme, and punctuation. They judged the merit of a poem on how difficult it was to understand. This study was conducted decades ago, but I wonder if we would find similar results if the study were carried out in today's grades 4 to 8 classrooms. All too often, I have observed students writing couplets or quatrains that make little sense but have impeccable rhyme schemes. These students devote so much energy to finding rhyming words that they lose track of what they want to say in their poems. Keeping track of the number of syllables and finding rhyming words may distract students from communicating their intended message.

Yet, if we encourage students to focus on meaning and playing with words, poetry will not be difficult for them. When students write list poems and free verse, for example, they do not have to get caught up in the demands of rhyme and rhythm schemes. Robert Frost (in Robertson 1997, p. 167) says that "writing free verse is like playing tennis with the net down." Just as it takes much less effort for tennis players to hit a ball onto the opponent's court when the net is down, it is easier for our students to say something worthwhile when writing poetry that is not constrained by rules for rhyme and meter. In this chapter, I present ideas for encouraging students to pay attention to words and ideas. I begin with a list of suggested avenues for inviting poetry writing in various content area subjects then move to teaching ideas for developing students' abilities to craft poems as they deepen their content area learning.

HELPING STUDENTS BECOME BETTER POETRY WRITERS

According to Georgia Heard (1998, p. 65) there are two types of tools that writers can use to craft poetry:

1. meaning tools (e.g., image, metaphor, line breaks, and titles)
2. music tools (e.g., rhyme, repetition and/or patterns, rhythm, and alliteration)

These tools are like the lines, colours, and shapes that visual artists use to create paintings. Just as artists try out thick, thin, wavy, or straight lines to see what effect they will have on the overall composition of a painting, poets play with various ways to break up phrases to determine how the flow and the meaning of their poetry will be affected. Helping students use these tools may involve identifying examples in published poetry, but that is only a small part of teaching the craft of poetry writing. Make sure to provide ample space for students to use these tools as they write poems that are meant to delight readers.

Experienced poets identify two essential creative skills :

1. selecting precise words
2. trimming phrases down to their essence

Poet Patrick Lane says, "Poets still pay attention to each word, you see." He goes even further, declaring that "most prose is sloppy, flabby poetry at best" (in Bowling 2002, p. 70). Lane's assertion here may seem extreme, but he certainly makes the point that poets are very selective in their word choices. Michael Ondaatje explains that he revises and shapes his poems in an effort to "remove all those extra clothes that were there" in his early drafts (in Bowling 2002, p. 34). These two poets' descriptions give a clear picture of poetry writing: the

IDEAS FOR WRITING POETRY ACROSS THE CURRICULUM

Social Studies
Have students:

- write a poem for two voices comparing the distinguishing features of early civilizations

- write a cinquain about historical figures who have contributed to the development of the country and the world (e.g., political figures, inventors)

Science
Have students:

- write a riddle about sounds in everyday life and how they are produced

- write a chant about energy conservation

Mathematics
Have students:

- write a rhyming couplet to help memorize multiplication basic facts

- write a question-and-answer poem consisting of probability problems and their answers

> How many times does a red
> End up in my hand
> When I tip the M and M bag?
>
> One in seven, my friend,
> Try it yourself.
>
> It's one in seven.

Art
Have students:

- write a free-verse poem describing a favourite painting or sculpture

- write a rhyming couplet that can be used as a title for a painting or sculpture that you have created

Health
Have students:

- write a haiku about healthy relationships with friends, family, and peers

- write a shape poem about healthy and not-so-healthy food choices

Music
Have students:

- rewrite the lyrics to well-known folk songs

- clap four or five bars in 2/4, 3/4, or 4/4 time; have them string words together, matching the rhythm you clap, to create a chant

craft of writing poetry involves ensuring that the writing is lean and free of unnecessary words.

This attention to word meanings is very likely to translate into deeper learning of the concepts you are teaching in your content classes. In the mini-lessons that follow, I provide suggestions to help students think about the words and ideas that arise from content area units as they write poetry.

Part I: Mini-Lessons to Teach Meaning and Music Tools

Mini-Lesson I.1: Experimenting with Line Breaks

Georgia Heard (1998, p. 84) says that poets work with the "tension between sound and silence"; they think about the words and the "silence between the words." The poem's rhythm is created not only in the accents and syllables of the words but also in the lines and where they are broken on the page. Line breaks might occur where readers would naturally take a breath or where poets want to emphasize certain words. Poets might change the pace of a poem or create tension by using a technique called *enjambment*, in which the natural rhythm or meaning of a line is interrupted by being carried onto the next line.

In this mini-lesson, have students play with sentences from a content area textbook or trade book, or from their own writing, to get a sense of how the meaning and rhythm change, depending on where the lines are broken. To support students in using line breaks in their poetry writing, I suggest copying BLM 5.1 onto an overhead transparency, then together experiment with where the line breaks could be placed. You might add, change, or cut words as you create a poem from these sentences. It is helpful to have students read aloud the results of the group efforts to see how the line breaks influence the way they read and the way they think about the ideas in the sentence. Have students trade their poems with a partner to compare and contrast what they have done and how the rhythms and meanings are different as a result of the different line breaks. In the example in BLM 5.2, where line breaks might occur in the sentence, the word *Mountains* in the second example is emphasized because it is alone on the line. We get a sense that the writer wants us to consider this word very carefully. Have students then either take additional sentences from a content area book to play with line breaks independently or write their own poems about an activity, experiment, field trip, interview, or observation.

Mini-Lesson I.2: Using Repetition of Words, Sounds, or Lines

David Booth and Bill Moore (2003) write that poems "make our ears sing" (p. 26). The "singing" is created by the sounds of individual words (e.g., using onomatopoeia—words that sound like the things they describe). Singing is also found within the sounds of words placed together (e.g.; *rhymes*—parts of words sound the same; alliteration—words in a phrase start with the same sound; *consonance*—words in a phrase or sentence have similar consonant sounds in the middle or at the end of the words; or *assonance*—words in a phrase or sentence have similar vowel sounds, but they may not rhyme). Sometimes the repetition of words or phrases brings out the musicality within poems. In this mini-lesson, draw students' attention to the sounds of the language in poems and invite them to use repeated sounds, words, or phrases to make their poems sing. Have students play around with the possibilities for using poets' tools, in this case the tool of repetition. The mini-lesson could start with a paragraph from a content area textbook or trade book on a topic. It could also start with a student's notes from reading a textbook or from a the student's activity, field trip, interview, or observation. In the example in BLM 5.3, the grade-7 student Ashif used notes taken from a presentation and a website to create the poem in BLM 5.4. He identified words related to his topic and other words that had initial, middle, and final sounds that he could use in his poem. He liked the sound of the word *nicotine* and decided to repeat it in his poem.

To support your students' use of the tool of repetition, you might make copies of a paragraph from a text you are using, double-spacing it to give students room to write. Invite students to underline words that are really important. Then ask them to think of words that rhyme with the underlined words that start with the same letter, or that have the same vowel or consonant sounds in the middle or at the end of the words. It is often helpful to use a dictionary to generate the words. As well, have students play around with words and phrases that they could repeat for emphasis. Ask them to keep these words in mind as they compose their poems, but their focus should be on saying something about the topic. They might use only one or two of the words from their list, or they might use many words. The goal is for them to play with repeated sounds and words but not to lose the sense of the poem for the sake of repeating sounds.

Mini-Lesson I.3: Creating Images of Concrete Experiences

Poets try to help readers "imagine, visualize, and, ultimately, bring [readers] closer to the experience of the poem" (Booth and Moore 2003, p. 64). In this mini-lesson, have students attempt to do just that—create visual images that help readers imagine the sounds, smells, and textures of the experiences communicated in their poetry. This mini-lesson works well following hands-on activities.

Shelbi, a grade-5 student, wrote the poem in BLM 5.5 following a field trip to a park to observe bugs. Ratiba, a grade-6 student, wrote about her experience working with pastels in art class (see BLM 5.6). Have students read the poem aloud. First ask them to enjoy its sounds and rhythms then to focus on the pictures that the words have created in their minds. They can draw or paint the pictures, or they can talk about them with a partner. Then have them focus on the words and phrases that the poets used to create their images.

Following the discussion, have students write their own poems. They might begin by writing words and phrases that capture a concrete experience that they have had in class or on a field trip, or they might plunge right into writing their poems. The phrases might simply be tools for remembering the experience, or they might end up in the poems.

Mini-Lesson I.4: Writing Titles

Titles usually give readers a sense of what a poem is about, but sometimes they might provide just enough information to create suspense or raise questions about the topic. Often, a title is the same as the first lines of a poem.

In this mini-lesson, have your students read through and identify how titles of published poetry contribute to the poems. Prepare by gathering published poetry (see the list on page 34 or draw from your own collection). Have students

POETRY COLLECTIONS FOR STUDENTS

General Collections

Booth, D. *'Til All the Stars Have Fallen*. Toronto: Kids Can Press, 1989.

Cullinan, B. (ed.) *A Jar of Tiny Stars: Poems by NCTE Award-Winning Poets*. Honesdale, PA: Boyds Mills Press, 1996.

Greenberg, J. *Heart to Heart: New Poems Inspired by Twentieth-Century American Art*. New York: Henry Abrams, 2001.

Hopkins, L.B. *Oh, No! Where Are My Pants? And Other Disasters: Poems*. New York: HarperCollins, 2005.

Prelutsky, J. (selected) *The 20th-Century Children's Poetry Treasury*. New York: Alfred A. Knopf, 1999.

Humorous Poems

Fitch, S. *If I Had a Million Onions*. Vancouver: Tradewind Books, 2005.

Grimes, N. *Thanks a Million*. New York: Greenwillow Books, 2006.

Lee, D. *Alligator Pie*. Toronto: Key Porter Kids, [1974] 2001.

_____ . *Garbage Delight: Another Helping*. Toronto: Key Porter Kids, 2002.

Lesynski, L. *Nothing Beats a Pizza*. Toronto: Annick Press, 2001.

_____ . *Cabbagehead*. Toronto: Annick Press, 2003.

Little, J. *Hey, World, Here I Am!* Toronto: Kids Can Press, 1998.

Scieszka, J. *Science Verse*. New York: Viking, 2004.

Silverstein, S. *Where the Sidewalk Ends: 30th-Anniversary Edition*. New York: HarperCollins, 2004.

Poems About the Natural World

Fleischman, P. *Joyful Noise: Poems for Two Voices*. New York: Harper & Row, 1988.

Florian, D. *Mammalabilia: Poems and Paintings*. San Diego: Harcourt Brace & Company, 2000.

George, K. *Hummingbird Nest: A Journal of Poems*. Orlando, FL: Harcourt, 2004.

Gottfried, M. *Good Dog*. New York: Alfred A. Knopf, 2005.

Nickel, B. *From the Top of a Grain Elevator*. Vancouver, BC: Beach Holme Publishing, 1999.

Sidman, J. *Song of the Water Boatman and Other Pond Poems*. Boston: Houghton Mifflin, 2005.

Singer, M. *Fireflies at Midnight*. New York: Atheneum Books for Young Readers, 2003.

form pairs and read five or six poems, recording the title and what the title contributes to the poem. For example, the titles of the water-bug poem in BLM 5.5 and the pastel crayon poem in BLM 5.6 summarize what the poems are about. Students can compare with other groups what they have found out about the contributions that titles make to poems.

Have your students then create two or three possible titles for their own poems. Because writers often are not entirely clear about what their poems will be about until they have written them, I recommend that titles be created after the poems are written. When students do this, they often end up discovering more about the topic.

Part II: Mini-Lessons for Staying Lean and Removing the Extra Layers

Mini-Lesson II.1: Creating a List Poem on Overhead Transparency Strips

Have students create a class poem by writing short phrases on strips of overhead transparencies. Work with students to arrange the plastic strips into a smoothly flowing poem that communicates what they have learned about a content area topic. This is the best activity I know of for fostering a frugal, discerning attitude toward choosing words. Because students write on small strips of acetate with wide-point overhead-transparency pens, they have no choice but to write a few well-chosen, meaning-laden words. For this reason, the activity is particularly effective for developing note-taking skills. I have seen this activity used with great success in every subject area from grades 4 to 8.

To prepare for this mini-lesson, cut up overhead transparencies into strips that are approximately 6 cm by 2 cm. Divide the class into groups of three students each. Distribute several of these strips and overhead pens to each group. Have copies of materials that students can read for gathering information about the content area topic. I generally ask younger students to read one or two paragraphs from trade books or textbooks on the topic and older students to read one or two pages. To prepare students from a grade-5 class who wrote the example in the BLM 5.7, I gave students five or six pages of advertisements from teen magazines (see BLM 5.7). Your students might also gather information from watching videos, completing hands-on activities, or participating in field trips. Have them write one idea from their reading, video, activity, or field trip on each overhead strip, using as few words as possible, perhaps just a noun and a verb. Place the strips on the overhead projector. Work alongside your students, reorganizing and combining phrases to create a poem that you are all happy with. You may decide as a group to create a phrase that can be repeated as a refrain, as well. Students can then create their own poems independently or in pairs.

Mini-Lesson II.2: Comparing and Contrasting Information in Two-Voice Poems

The two-voice poem works well when you want students to compare and contrast information on two topics. I use Paul Fleischman's (1988) *Joyful Noise: Poems for Two Voices* as a model. To gather and organize information for the poems, students should complete a compare/contrast chart (see BLM 3.12). The example shown in BLM 5.8 can be used to demonstrate how students might create a poem for two voices from notes organized in the compare/contrast chart. It shows how two grade-8 students wrote a poem for their social studies unit on Canadian history. Point out to students that the two voices sometimes speak together, as indicated by placing the phrase in the middle of the page. They take turns reading characteristics that are unique to each father of Confederation. When the voices speak together, they are speaking of characteristics that they have in common. When I use this example, I point out how the students combined some information from their notes on the compare/contrast chart (see BLM 3.12) and decided not to use some of the other information. I point out how the boys used keywords from their compare/contrast chart and didn't rewrite everything from the chart in their poem. Then, using compare/contrast chart notes for the topic we are studying, my students and I together write a poem together as a class. I have my students follow up by writing their own compare/contrast poems.

Mini-Lesson II.3: Distilling Poems from Paragraphs

In addition to helping students develop their poetry-writing skills, this mini-lesson is an excellent activity for developing note-taking skills. Start by making an overhead transparency of a paragraph from a content book. I recommend that you think aloud, demonstrating to your students how to select the words that are essential to communicating the gist of the paragraph. Shape those words into a poem. (See BLM 5.9 for an example written by grade-6 students.)

Mini-Lesson II.4: Writing from Content Area Vocabulary Lists

Our refrigerator, like those of many of my friends, has a scattering of words on magnets that we put together to create silly, provocative, and/or profound messages. This mini-lesson works in the same way as the refrigerator-magnet word game works. Have students create poems from a collection of words that are important to the topic under study. As they write their poems, they will be thinking about the concepts and applying what they have learned. The activity is great for building vocabulary as well as for developing students' poetry-writing repertoires.

I suggest that you introduce this mini-lesson by composing a poem together with your students. Base the poem on vocabulary from the unit of study. I find it helpful to include nouns, verbs, and adjectives in the list, and I also include words that students can have fun with that are unrelated to the content area topic, which I call *wild words*. These wild words are taken from other poems, songs, or stories and can be used in the same way as wild cards in a card game are. See BLM 5.10 for lists of nouns, verbs, adjectives, and wild words, and the poem created to explain the geometry concepts. The grade-4 students who created this poem added words and modified the forms (e.g., changed verbs to nouns).

WORKS CITED

Booth, D., and B. Moore. *Poems Please: Sharing Poetry with Children*. 2nd ed. Toronto: Pembroke, 2003.

Bowling, T. *Where the Words Come From: Canadian Poets in Conversation*. Roberts Creek, BC: Nightwood Editions, 2002.

Corrigan, P. "Handing Down Knowledge: A Poetic Apprenticeship." *Voices from the Middle* 10.2 (2002), 33–37.

Cullinan, B.E., M.C. Scala, and V.C. Schroder. *Three Voices: An Invitation to Poetry across the Curriculum*. Toronto: Pembroke, 1995.

Fleischman, P. *Joyful Noise: Poems for Two Voices*, Harper & Row, 1988.

Heard, G. *Awakening the Heart: Exploring Poetry in Elementary and Middle School.* Portsmouth, NH: Heinemann, 1998.

Robertson, C. (ed.) *The Dictionary of Quotations.* Hertfordshire, UK: Wordsworthy Editions, 1997.

Strenski, E., and N.G. Esposito. "The Poet, the Computer, and the Classroom." *College English* 42 (1980), 142–150.

Wooldridge, S.G. *Peomcrazy: Freeing Your Life with Words.* New York: Three Rivers Press, 1996.

The drive to story is basic in all human beings. Stories shape our lives and our culture—we cannot live without them.

—David Booth and Bob Barton

Writing Narrative Across the Curriculum

Chapter **6**

WHY WRITE NARRATIVE IN CONTENT AREAS?

David Booth and Bob Barton make it clear (above) that stories are essential to being human. We all have a basic need to organize and make sense of our experiences through narrative. Stories help us give structure "to our mountain of memories and emotions, making sense and giving cohesion to our lives" (2002, p. 8). When we read and write stories, we come to know ourselves and discover what contributions we might make to our world. The stories we write and read help us understand what is and envision what might be. Daily, we use stories to build relationships with others, finding that the stories of others entertain us and open our perspectives on the world. Through the ages, humans have used stories to teach and shape others' behaviour. Today, our students encounter stories of their peers, family members, and community members while getting ready for school, while riding the bus, walking to school, or making their way through the school hallways. They not only hear the stories of the people they know, but they also have stories available to them from every corner of the world every day. Newspapers, magazines, television, radio, and Internet information sources use narrative to convey social, scientific, or political information. Often, these stories follow individuals whose lives are affected by the major news events of each week. These local stories give meaning to the seemingly abstract events that are far removed from the experiences of many of our students.

We cannot deny that stories are part of our students' worlds beyond the school curriculum. Why, then, would we not be able to find space for narrative within the content area curricula? Social studies, health, science, art, mathematics, and music are all about people, ideas, events, as well as the natural world and the world that we humans have created. Gordon Wells (1984, p. 194) tells us that there is plenty of room for narrative. He explains that storying is

NARRATIVE FORMS: A SHORT LIST

realistic fiction	cartoons	historical fiction
mystery	science fiction	fantasy
ballad	biography	diary
script for a play, film, radio show	script for a puppet show	folk tale
myth	legend	fable

an activity that pervades all aspects of learning. . . . Stories are one of the most effective ways of making one's own interpretation of events and ideas available to others. Through the exchange of stories, therefore, teachers and students can share their understandings of a topic. . . . In this sense, stories and storying are relevant in all areas of the curriculum.

We add a personal dimension to curriculum content by inviting students to write stories about their learning. Students use narrative structures to breathe life into the concepts and ideas that curriculum documents identify as key learning objectives. Content knowledge becomes more relevant and understandable when connected to the experiences of story characters. In addition, familiar and beloved narrative structures (e.g., those that have an introduction and an initiating event leading to conflict that gets more intense until the protagonist solves the problem) provide dependable frameworks for pulling the content area knowledge together into a cohesive whole. I found this to be the case with students writing in grade-6 and grade-8 science classes. Most students wrote narratives when given the choice to use any genre to show what they had learned about simple machines. They told me that they found narrative writing easier and more enjoyable than poetry or non-narrative forms. (For a short list of narrative forms, see chart above.)

In spite of students' familiarity with the narrative genre, there are still challenges in writing narrative across the curriculum. In this chapter, I present three activities that you might use to address students' need for assistance in weaving content knowledge into their stories. In addition, I present ideas for writing narrative across the curriculum and some mini-lessons for helping students develop character, plot, and style as they write engaging stories at the same time as they extend their content area knowledge.

HELPING STUDENTS TO BECOME BETTER NARRATIVE WRITERS AND LEARN CONTENT

Make sure that your students have an authentic purpose for finding out as much as they can about a topic when they write stories in content areas. If they are writing about characters in a particular historical period, for example, they need information about the homes, food, entertainment, clothing, and family structures of the time.

IDEAS FOR WRITING NARRATIVE ACROSS THE CURRICULUM

Social Studies

Have students:

- write a series of diary entries telling a story of the everyday life of a particular group of people who are identified in the curriculum

- write a time-slip fantasy about a character from today's world who goes back in time to a setting from the social studies curriculum

Science

Have students:

- write an adventure story showing how characters use simple machines to survive

- write an autobiography of a stream

Mathematics

Have students:

- write a mystery in which the detective must use what students have learned in a measurement unit to solve the crime

- write a script for a radio play that tells the story of a character who gains or loses large amounts of something; have students demonstrate what they have learned about adding and subtracting four-digit numbers in their story

Art

Have students:

- write a story about a character who walks into a painting of their choice; have them consider how the colours, lines (e.g., smooth, flowing, horizontal, sharp, jagged, vertical) and textures contribute to the way the character acts, talks, and feels when she/he gets inside

- write a science fiction, fantasy, realistic fiction, or historical fiction story about a painter, showing what he/she knows about primary, secondary, and tertiary colours

Health

Have students:

- write a short play about characters who apply what they have learned about dealing with peer pressure related to substance use and abuse

- write a humorous or serious story (it could take the form of a cartoon) about a babysitting event showing what they have learned about caring for young children

Music

Have students:

- write a biography of a musical instrument, describing its history, construction, and use (e.g., a historical instrument such as the sackbut or the instruments that the students play in class)

- write new words to familiar melodies, using their knowledge of rhythm to ensure that the new text fits with the melody; the new words should tell a story

Part I: Mini-Lessons for Weaving Content Area Knowledge into Stories

Communicating content area knowledge through narrative is one of the more difficult writing tasks our students can take up. They have read and listened to enough stories to know that readers do not appreciate wading through a pedantic litany of facts. Their sights are set on the characters and their actions. Yet, if our students focus only on the story, they might not be deepening their learning of the content area concepts and perspectives. In my experience with students writing narrative in science, they are more likely to sacrifice content area information than they will sacrifice story detail. They usually have a strong sense of how stories work and want to entertain their audience.

When planning learning activities to help students weave content information into their narratives, I applaud these intentions and generally do not want to discourage them. However, when writing in content areas, students must keep in mind the equally important goal to learn content area concepts. Some students need support managing story and content demands.

Mini-Lesson I.1: Adapting Familiar Story Lines and Giving Examples

In this mini-lesson, have students assess the narrative produced by Craig, a grade-8 student, given in BLM 6.1. It was prepared in response to an assignment in which the student was to demonstrate what he knew about mechanical advantage, pulleys, levers, and gears in the genre of his choice. He made the task more manageable, as well as humorous and entertaining, by adapting a familiar story, Charles Dickens's *A Christmas Carol*. By using a tale upon which to base his own story, he could concentrate on creating new twists that incorporated the science information. Craig included the terminology from his science classes but has not given specific examples to demonstrate clearly what each term means. Discuss the story using the following questions as a starting point:

- Where do you see evidence in this story that the writer included information from his science class?
- What four science concepts does the story talk about? What do you learn about the four concepts?
- What questions are unanswered? What could the writer have done to give readers a better understanding of what the science terms mean?
- Summarize the plot of the story. Is it familiar to you?
- What did Craig do to make it easier to write a story about the four science concepts?
- What did Craig do to make the story entertaining? What else could he have done?

Following the discussion, have students look at the notes they have taken of the content area concepts they are to demonstrate in a narrative. Ask them to think about how they might adapt a familiar story line to suit their content area purposes. Of course, they might also create their own plots. In any case, students should strive to give examples in their stories of the concepts rather than just use the content vocabulary.

Mini-Lesson I.2: Using Plot to Communicate Content Area Knowledge

This mini-lesson on using plot to communicate content area knowledge is useful for giving students who want to create their own plots rather than do a twist on a familiar story; they might find the mystery genre useful for communicating content area information. The content area concepts can be used to solve the mystery or can be part of the mystery. The example shown in BLM 6.2 was written by Caitlin, a grade-8 student from the same class as Craig. She used drawings and description to communicate information about levers and pulleys. The mystery provides a context for using these simple machines. Conduct a class discussion about Caitlin's story, using the following questions as a starting point:

- Where do you see evidence that Caitlin has included information from her science class in her story? What contributions do the science concepts make to the plot?

- What do you learn about the concepts when you read this story?

- What questions are left unanswered? What could Caitlin have done to give readers a better understanding of what the science terms mean?

- What did Caitlin do to make the story entertaining? What else could she have done?

- How might you use a mystery to write about the concepts you have just learned? Would the mystery be solved by using the concepts or would the concepts be part of the mystery? If a mystery would not work, what other type of story might work better?

Following the discussion, students could look at the notes they have taken about the content area concepts they are to incorporate in a narrative. They would consider how they might use the mystery genre to suit their content area purposes or they could choose another genre that would be more suitable.

Mini-Lesson I.3: Using Character and Setting to Communicate Content Area Knowledge

This mini-lesson, on using character and setting to communicate content area knowledge, is a variation of the previous two, as it shows students how one student, Jessica, has integrated social studies information about the lifestyles of two classes of people in ancient Greece through characters' interactions and through descriptions of where they live (see BLM 6.3). Conduct a discussion of Jessica's story using the following questions as a starting point:

- Where do you see evidence that Jessica has included information from her social studies class in her story?

- What do you learn about the lifestyles of the wealthy class, the free labourers, and the slaves?

- Describe the characters and the setting. How did Jessica teach readers about the lifestyles of people in ancient Greece through her story?

- What questions are left unanswered? What could Jessica have done to give readers a better understanding of the lifestyles of the three groups of people who lived in ancient Greece?
- What kind of information can be communicated through describing characters and setting?
- What did Jessica do to make her story entertaining? What else do you think she could have done?

Following the discussion, have students look at their notes about the content area concepts they intend to demonstrate in a narrative. They should determine whether it would be possible to communicate the information through the setting and the characters.

Part II: Mini-Lessons for Developing Characters, Plot, and Style

Donald Graves (1994, p. 304) observed that, in many students' stories, the "characters exist for the plot." Students often write their characters into plots that mirror events in their lives or those drawn from television, movies, or video games. They frequently use a pronoun to refer to the character or may introduce ubiquitous characters, such as the "tall, blonde-haired girl" (these characters show up every year in countless grade-6 stories on provincial and state writing tests). Yet, as Ralph Fletcher (1993, p. 56) writes, "character remains pre-eminent. The characters contain the crucial human link, that element of human destiny, for the reader to identify with." To become better fiction writers, our students must go beyond referring to a character as 'he,' 'she,' or 'I'. They must go beyond using a stereotypical physical description again and again. The first two mini-lessons in this section are designed to help support students to develop their characters. In the first one, I have presented a planning framework that helps students think about personality traits for their characters. In the second, I suggest that students analyze how published authors use dialogue. Students can start developing a list of ways they can write dialogue that develops character and moves plot forward.

Mini-Lesson II.1: Allowing Characters to Lead the Way

In the past, I asked my elementary students to begin planning their stories by thinking about the plot. I had them fill planning pages with rectangles and circles and write what the initiating event would be, how the characters would be thwarted at every turn as they tried to resolve the conflict, and what actions would ultimately lead to resolution. These plot-structure charts ended up as plot-structure ruts. Many students rewrote the plot-structure chart as a story, and their stories turned out not to be character driven.

This approach clearly lacked the flexibility for students to be creative. In rethinking my approach to supporting students in writing narratives, I drew on the recommendations of published authors. Many say that they start writing their narratives by getting to know their characters. Certain characters will do only certain things, so knowing the characters is important in developing the whole story.

Now I suggest giving students the option of using a framework when thinking about potential characters for their narratives (see BLM 6.4). Students do not have to use the framework if they already have ideas for their characters; the framework is just a tool for those who need support. Have students answer the questions in this BLM to create their characters. They need not answer every question in the chart; some questions might be more appropriate than others for the characters the students want to create. Each question about a character has the potential for determining how the plot will develop. For example, questions about what stands out about the characters and about the characters' problems, motivations, and/or goals will likely be helpful in determining the initiating events for the plot. The characters' personalities, their strengths and weaknesses, or their unique physical features may provide ideas for how the characters will interact with each other to create or help resolve the conflict.

Mini-Lesson II.2: Developing Characters and Plot Through Dialogue

Dialogue is one of the hardest parts of writing a story. My past elementary and my current university students and I try to write dialogue that is as natural as possible. We try to weave it into the narration seamlessly, to make sure that what characters say is consistent with their actions and intentions. It is a tall order. If

ANNOTATED LIST OF BOOKS PROVIDING MODELS FOR DIALOGUE

Ho, M. *The Clay Marble*. New York: Farrar, Straus and Giroux, 1993. [The dialogue on pages 3 and 4 introduces the characters and the context of life in Cambodia in 1980. In this story, a 12-year old girl and her family flee their war-torn Cambodian village and make their way to a refugee camp on the Thai-Cambodian border.]

Lawrence, M. *The Gladiators from Capua*. London, UK: Orion Children's Books, 2004. [Students might find it interesting that the dialogue is enclosed in single quotation marks, because the book was published in the United Kingdom. The short, snappy dialogue on pages 29-30 moves the story along and establishes the characters' roles. This mystery story is set in Rome at the time of Emperor Titus.]

L'Engle, M. *A Wind in the Door*. New York: Farrar, Straus and Giroux, 1973. [On pages 3-5, characters and their idiosyncrasies are introduced through dialogue. The adventures in this science-fiction story take readers into outer space and the world of a mitochondrion.]

Sachs, M. *The Bears' House*. New York: Puffin, 1971. [On pages 63 and 64, Miss Thompson, Fran Ellen's teacher, asks questions about things that seem out of place in the household, and Fran Ellen does her best to answer truthfully without arousing her teacher's suspicion. This book is about relationships, imagined and real, in the life of a grade-4 girl who, because of the failings of the adults in her home life, takes on care-giving roles that demand far more than a 10-year-old should have to assume.]

Yee, P. *Dead Man's Gold and Other Stories*. Toronto: Groundwood, 2002. [The dialogue on pages 13 and 14 establishes the context for the story. There are some instances of characters thinking aloud, as well. The ghost stories are written in the style of traditional Chinese folktales. They tell of Chinese immigrants making new lives for themselves in North America.]

Yep, L. *The Traitor: Golden Mountain Chronicles*. New York: HarperCollins, 2003. [Action and dialogue are skillfully woven together on pages 206 and 207. This story, narrated by fictional characters, tells of the true-life 1885 massacre of Chinese miners who were hired to replace striking miners in Rock Springs, Wyoming.]

we use dialogue too often, or if a conversation goes on for too long, we run the risk of slowing down the story's progress.

Published authors wrestle with the same problems. Our students can learn a lot about writing dialogue by analyzing published writing. Analysis helps them develop a repertoire of techniques for their own writing of dialogue. In this mini-lesson, have students work with a partner or in a small group to read the dialogue from books that they are reading, or from the annotated list found on page 45. Have them act out the roles of characters to bring the dialogue to life. Then, have them identify:

- the kind of information the dialogue provides
- what kinds of words and expressions make the dialogue seem natural
- what is written before and after the dialogue so that it seems to fit well with the rest of the passage
- how many lines the dialogue takes up
- how many characters are involved in the conversation
- how the author structures the dialogue (e.g., what words the author uses for *said*, how often the author attaches the speaker's name to the dialogue, how the dialogue is indented)

To develop an extensive list of ways to use dialogue to develop plot and character, have students put their notes together with those of the rest of the class. Then have them take a look at their own narrative writing and think about where dialogue would be useful in developing characters or plot. Ask them to think about how much information the dialogue should provide, who will be involved, and for how long it should go on, for example. Use BLM 6.5 to record students' analyses of the dialogue they read, or as an overhead transparency if you wish to do this activity as a whole class.

Mini-Lesson II.3: The Challenge of Details

Details, details, details! Every standardized scoring guide for writing seems to have some mention of the use of detail and description. Details are important to give readers a sense of what the writer is trying to say. Many students seem intent on giving only the bare bones of the plot so that they and their readers do not get bogged down in details. Too little detail, however, makes the reader work too hard to figure out what is really happening and who the characters really are. They argue that too much detail makes a story boring. It certainly is possible to have too many details that end up distracting readers from the main story. Sometimes an overly detailed story is almost insulting to readers, never mind boring. As readers, we like to work out some things for ourselves. The overly detailed story is like a movie with characters who tell each other what they are going to do before they take action. They voice their opinions of each other, for example, leaving nothing for the viewer to figure out. The trick is to include enough detail so that readers can follow what is going on and also to leave some gaps so that readers can use their background knowledge and experience to create their own images and impressions. Roland Barthes and

Richard Miller (1975) call this "writerly text." Help students recognize writerly text by presenting an example of a bare-bones version of a paragraph from published fiction. Use the example in BLM 6.6, or create a threadbare version of a story that you use in your subject area. Ask students to work with you or have them work in small groups to revise the sentence in this BLM by adding details to show readers what it was like for Chu, the character in Paul Yee's short story "Spirit of the Railway." Then have them read the paragraph that Paul Yee himself wrote (see BLM 6.6) and discuss what it means to add details that help readers picture what a situation is like for characters. Ask the following questions:

- What images do you have of winter from the single sentence? From Paul Yee's paragraph? From your paragraph?
- What details did Paul Yee use to help you imagine what the winter was like for Chu? What details did you use?

You might do the same with an "overstuffed" paragraph from published fiction. Use the example written by Yee or find an overstuffed version from your choice of fiction. Ask students what information is helpful in creating images and what they might cut because the excessive detail is getting in the way of the story.

Have students revise the extremely detailed paragraph in BLM 6.7, then conduct a discussion with the following questions as a starting point:

- From the long version, what images do you have of the work that Chu and the crew did? From Paul Yee's paragraph (in BLM 6.7)? From your paragraph?
- What details did Paul Yee use (in BLM 6.7) to help you imagine the work that Chu and the crew did?
- Which details did you keep and which did you cut in the overstuffed paragraph? Why did you keep those details and not others?

Have students read to peers what they wrote and get feedback on where more detail is needed and the places where too many details get in the way of the message.

Mini-Lesson II.4: Beginnings (Leads) and Endings

The first challenge of writing narratives is determining how the stories should begin. Writers have many choices. Of the many possibilities for leads, a writer might use a particular lead to describe a character's ordinary life and what happens to change her/his life. Or the writer might use it to create a mood or foreshadow an event. One important consideration in writing story leads is to decide where to start the story in the chronology of events. Stories do not have to begin at the beginning. Sometimes more suspense is created when a writer starts at the end or somewhere in the middle and uses flashback to bring readers forward in time.

A second challenge is how to resolve the problem presented in the story and how much farther the story line should move after the problem is resolved. Conduct a discussion to help students write resolutions to the problems they created for their characters by using the following questions as a starting point:

PICTURE BOOKS THAT WEAVE CONTENT INTO NARRATIVES

Burleigh, R. *Seurat and La Grande Jatte: Connecting the Dots.* New York: H.N. Abrams, 2004. [This biography of Georges Seurat's life highlights one of his best known paintings, *A Sunday on La Grande Jatte,* and introduces readers to pointillism.]

Kaplan, W. *One More Border: The True Story of One Family's Escape From War-Torn Europe.* Toronto: Groundwood, 1998. [In the spring of 1939, the Jewish Kaplan family flees Lithuania, ending up in Canada.]

Laurie, P. *Lost Treasure of the Inca.* Honesdale, PA: Boyds Mills Press,1999. [The author tells the tale of his search for lost Inca gold, ransom for an Inca king, on a trek through mountainous Ecuador. Woven through the story is information about the Inca.]

Marin, R. *Oscar: The Life and Music of Oscar Peterson.* Toronto: Groundwood, 2004. [This biography of Canadian jazz musician Oscar Peterson introduces jazz concepts, such as improvisation.]

Scieszka, J. *Math Curse.* New York: Viking, 1995. [A school-aged girl is cursed when her math teacher informs the class that "you can think of almost everything as a math problem."]

Webb, S. *Looking for Seabirds: Journal from an Alaskan Voyage.* Boston, MA: Houghton Mifflin, 2004. [The author chronicles her month-long expedition to the Aleutian Islands in Alaska as she counts seabirds, whose population density can help gauge the ocean's health.]

- Should the protagonist deal with the problem himself/herself or enlist the help of others?

- Should all the readers' questions about how the protagonist fares be answered? Should a few questions be left unanswered so that readers can decide for themselves what happens?

- What should happen to the antagonists? Should they be shown forgiveness or mercilessly punished (or something in between)?

- Should the protagonist resume the ordinary patterns of life that were in place before the story began, or should she/he move on to another setting as a changed person?

Published authors have responded to these questions without digging their characters into such deep holes that mass destruction is the only way to end the story. (Many students resort to such endings!) Published authors can provide students with a repertoire of ways to answer questions about ending narratives.

In this mini-lesson, have students analyze how authors of picture books begin and end their stories. I suggest using picture books because they can be read more quickly for the purpose of the mini-lesson. Also, our students will be writing short stories, not novels, for their assignments. I find that students get bogged down in complicated twists and turns of the plot when they model their plots after those in novels or movies. These students tire of writing the stories before they can move the story line toward a believable conclusion. Provide your students with picture books as examples of how they might move characters through an event in just a few pages. Have them read a picture book with a partner. (See the list of picture books above, which can be used for this mini-lesson.) These books both convey information and tell a story. You may also want to use books from your own collection. Have students respond to the questions in BLM 6.8 to analyze the lead and the ending of each story. Then have them compare their analysis with those of their peers. They can then draw on their growing repertoire of possibilities for leads and endings when writing their own narratives.

Mini-Lesson II.5: Showing and Not Telling—Using Films

When we explain to students the concept of *showing* rather than *telling* readers what a scene, person, or thing is like, we often use phrases like "give specific examples to help readers create visual images" or "bring readers onto the scene so they can see what is happening." An effective way to give students a sense of what is meant by "showing and not telling" is by analyzing video clips. Every time we watch a movie, we are being shown what the characters are like. Their actions, responses to one another, and their dialogue all give clues about the characters' nature.

My favourite video that depicts showing and not telling is called *The Sandlot* (1993). It appeals to students of all ages because of its loveable characters and humorous story line (the gender stereotyping, however, is an issue that you might need to take up with your students). Information about baseball and baseball heroes is woven artfully into the story. One character stumbles into awkward situations because of his lack of knowledge of the game. Other characters fill in the gaps in the main character's knowledge, sometimes helpfully and at other times disdainfully. I recommend showing a short clip of the video (about 10 minutes, thus avoiding copyright infringement) in which the personality of a character is demonstrated through his/her actions and conversations with others. Conduct a discussion about the video by using the following questions as a starting point:

- How would you describe the character?
- What did the character do or say to give you this impression?
- What did others do or say to the character?

Then have students write a script for the video clip, including information about the characters' actions and what they say to each other. Or have them read their own writing with a partner to determine where they are showing readers what a character, scene, or event is like and where revisions are needed to strengthen their writing.

WORKS CITED

Barthes, R., and R. Miller (trans.). *S/Z*. London, UK: Cape, 1975.

Barton, B., and D. Booth. *Stories in the Classroom: Storytelling, Reading Aloud and Roleplaying with Children*. Toronto: Pembroke, 1990.

Booth, D., and B. Barton. *Story Works: How Teachers Can Use Shared Stories in the New Curriculum*. Toronto: Pembroke, 2002.

Fletcher, R. *What a Writer Needs*. Portsmouth, NH: Heinemann, 1993.

Graves, D. *A Fresh Look at Writing*. Portsmouth, NH: Heinemann, 1994.

The Sandlot. Dir. David M. Evans. Twentieth Century Fox. 1993.

Wells, G. *The Meaning Makers: Children Learning Language and Using Language to Learn*. Portsmouth, NH: Heinemann, 1986.

Punctuation adds texture to language. It's like feeling a fine handmade cloth with our eyes closed; we feel the nap, the bumps, the weave. It's good not to worry too much about punctuation in the beginning. But after a while the punctuation becomes part of what we're trying to say.

—Georgia Heard

Teaching Writing Conventions Across the Curriculum

Chapter 7

YES, WE ALL TEACH WRITING CONVENTIONS

I don't have to worry about spelling, punctuation, and grammar. This isn't language arts class." How often have we heard students make this proclamation? They seem to associate writing conventions with a subject area rather than with generally effective written communication. I have found that many students view writing conventions as a tightly woven net that is cast over their writing, trapping them in rules and expectations. In their minds, the language arts teacher is the only teacher who has licence to cast that net. It is clear that these students are not looking at writing conventions through the same lens as Georgia Heard (above)! She sees punctuation as an interwoven part of any written communication. Punctuation is not a trap for writers but rather a tool that adds to and becomes part of the fabric of a piece of writing. Because of their widespread use, writing conventions serve as signposts for readers. They provide familiar ground for understanding what the writing says. One challenge for teachers in all subject areas is to show students how their use of conventions helps readers understand the writing. As I have shown in chapter 1, writing conventions vary with the genre and the context. Conventions expected and accepted by peer audiences in text messaging and emailing differ from those of formal essays written for a social studies class, for example. Emailers use abbreviations and punctuation that would not be acceptable, and perhaps not even understood, by a teacher audience. Similarly, the weave of conventions used in poetry writing is generally much looser than that in essays. Yet, there are exceptions. A sonnet, for example, has a tight weave of syllabic expectations that students might find difficult to manipulate. Helping students understand how communication expectations and needs vary with the context is a second challenge for teachers.

In this chapter, I present suggestions for teaching writing conventions with the belief that the responsibility for teaching and assessing writing conventions falls on the shoulders of teachers in all subject areas, not just the language arts teacher. It is important to remember, though, that being responsible for teaching writing conventions does not mean you will have a systematic program that covers all possible grammar, punctuation, and spelling rules. Instead, you will focus instruction on the conventions that appear again and again in students' writing and that students show they are struggling with.

If you teach language arts in addition to content area subjects, you can give mini-lessons on writing conventions and proofreading to the whole class or make them part of small-group writers workshops. You can also conduct on-the-spot mini-lessons with students. This can be done in conjunction with consultation during writers workshop or during content area classes. If you teach only content area classes, you might teach one or two mini-lessons to the whole class or to small groups during the weeks that are devoted to writing. On-the-spot mini-lessons that respond to individual students' needs are also helpful during these times. In addition, it is worthwhile communicating with your colleagues who teach language arts to let them know of pervasive convention errors in student writing. It works well to find a way to collaborate in addressing these trouble areas. Language arts teachers may also be interested in addressing the problems by conducting mini-lessons in their own writers workshops.

TEACHING WRITING CONVENTIONS

Two questions frequently arise when I read students' writing that is hard to understand because of convention errors: (1) What does the writing show about the writer's understanding of spelling, punctuation, and grammar? (2) How can I help the writer expand and refine her/his repertoire of writing conventions? I also think about how I can help the writer recognize the relationship between writing conventions and readers' understanding, and how I can guide students in developing proofreading and editing skills.

This chapter is divided into two sections, accordingly. The first section, directed toward expanding and refining students' repertoires, makes suggestions for teaching writing conventions. The second section provides techniques for developing students' proofreading and editing skills.

Part I: Mini-Lessons for Direct Teaching of Writing Conventions

Reading and writing are the foundations for learning about the effective use of writing conventions. Whether or not they recognize it, readers do possess an understanding of conventional uses of spelling, punctuation, and grammar. Their reading creates visual memories of conventional spellings, sentence structures, and punctuation that they can recreate in their own writing. Jan Turbill's (2000) story about her nephew shows the importance of encouraging students' attention to writing conventions when they read. Her nephew spelled technical terms correctly but often misspelled everyday words when he wrote papers for his university courses. He explained that when he read technical texts he consciously learned spellings of words that he planned to use in his own writing. He looked carefully at the technical words to work out their meanings. He knew that his computer's spell-checking program would not catch those words, so it was up to him to check the spellings of the technical words. He did not pay attention to those words that were more commonly used and caught by a spell-checking program.

Like Jan Turbill's nephew, our students use what they have noticed to make hypotheses about spelling, grammar, and punctuation. Writing provides space for testing out the hypotheses to see how they help or hinder readers' understanding. Having many opportunities to write across the curriculum allows students to apply their hypotheses about writing conventions to a wide range of genres and contexts. Our teaching of writing conventions does not stop at creating space for lots of attentive reading and abundant time for writing, however. Some students need explicit instruction to help them recognize the conventions as they read, then they need guided practice to apply their learning as they write. I generally use two types of lessons when teaching writing conventions and proofreading skills. One is *inductive teaching*, which involves investigations of the use of the convention in published writing, analyses of the similarities in the ways that writers have used the convention, followed by making generalizations about using the convention. The second is *deductive teaching*, which starts with an explanation of a convention rule and is followed by a search for examples that confirm the rule. Each type of lesson culminates with students applying the rules in their own writing.

The inductive lessons given in mini-lessons I.1 and I.2 in this chapter focus on helping students with common convention errors. The deductive lessons in mini-lessons II.1 and II.2 help teach proofreading and editing skills. The techniques in all four mini-lessons can be applied to teaching any convention or writing skill that students find difficult. Following a mini-lesson, either with the whole class, with small groups, or with individual students, make sure to reinforce the learning. I find that the best way to do this is to ask students to find uses of the convention in their own writing. Have them consider where they have used the convention to clarify readers' understanding and where their incorrect use of the convention obscures the meaning. You might give further reinforcement when you assess the student's writing or provide feedback. In these instances, you would highlight where the student's use of the convention helped understanding and where it hindered.

Mini-Lesson I.1: Inductive Teaching to Differentiate Words that Sound and/or Look Similar but Have Different Meanings

Students at all levels confuse words that look or sound very similar but have different meanings. Henriksson (2001, p. 13), for example, found the following error in a college student's paper: "Alexander the Great conquered Persia, Egypt, and Japan. Sadly, he died with no hairs." Such errors, while humorous to readers who have a good sense of what the writer really wanted to say, can be embarrassing for writers. The most commonly confused words are:

- there/their/they're
- to/too/two
- your/you're

- except/accept
- then/than
- effect/affect
- its/it's

You could carry out an inductive lesson focusing on any of these sets of words. BLM 7.1 treats the use of the contraction *it's* and the possessive form of it—*its*. Have students look for examples of each word in the poem, determining what words *its* and *it's* replace in each phrase. *It's* replaces *it is*, and *its* replaces *the solid's* in the first two examples. As well, they could do the same with any piece of writing appropriate to what you're teaching. They might also sort the examples into two piles, one in which *it's* is used and the other where *its* is used. Then have students write a generalization to help them remember the differences between the two words and then apply what they have learned by proofreading and editing their writing.

Mini-Lesson I.2: Inductive Teaching of Commas

The rules for using commas are not hard and fast. I find that some editors steadfastly apply certain rules with no exceptions, while other editors bend some rules and apply others more vigorously. In any case, the rules were created to make it easier for readers to understand the writing. Clear communication is the basic rule for using commas.

In this mini-lesson, have students investigate how published writers use commas. Have them look at the patterns of comma usage to determine principles for using commas in their own writing. You can repeat this mini-lesson for different types of writing so students come to recognize the roles that commas play in fiction, informational text, and poetry. To start the mini-lesson, make copies of BLM 7.2 and distribute them to each student or group of students. After the students have compared their notes with the rest of the class, draw up a class set of rules for using commas. Use BLM 7.3 to help students assess where the writer's use of commas helped or confused communication. Then, have them proofread and edit their own writing according to the rules they have established.

Part II: Mini-Lessons for Developing Proofreading Skills

How do the punctuation, spelling, and grammar of a piece of writing influence readers' understanding? We want students to ask themselves this question as they proofread their writing. Model techniques and ways of thinking that students can use when proofreading and editing their writing.

Mini-Lesson II.1: Deductive Teaching of Proofreading Skills for Spelling

In Jan Turbill's (2000) research, 200 teachers read an article containing misspelled words and identified a number of strategies that they used when proofreading. Demonstrate these strategies on a piece of your own writing, a piece from one of your students, or the piece in BLM 7.4. Copy the piece onto an overhead transparency so the whole class can see as you circle the misspelled words. Voice your thoughts about how you know when a word is misspelled. Here are some strategies you might use as you circle the misspelled words (adapted from Turbill 2000, p. 212):

- the word looks wrong
- the word does not follow particular spelling rules you know

Here are some strategies you might use for correcting the spelling:

- read on to see if the word is used somewhere else
- reread the word to see if the meaning is correct for the spelling
- use a dictionary
- sound out syllables

Mini-Lesson II.2: Deductive Teaching—Using Editing Symbols

In this mini-lesson, introduce simple editing symbols to help students become independent proofreaders and editors. The first step is to introduce students to the symbols that editors use (see BLM 7.5). Demonstrate how students would use the symbols by editing the piece in BLM 7.6, or a piece of your choice, on the overhead projector. After the demonstration, invite students to use the symbols to proofread unedited writing samples. They may use their own writing or the material in BLM 7.7.

WORKS CITED

Heard, G. *Writing Toward Home*. Portsmouth, NH: Heinemann, 1995.

Henriksson, A. *Non Campus Mentis: World History According to College Students*. New York: Workman Publishing, 2001.

Turbill, J. "Developing a Spelling Conscience." *Language Arts* 77.3 (2000), 209–217.

To young people, the Net has become wallpaper, shamelessly blending with the social spaces they inhabit in the real world.

—Media Awareness Network

Teaching Writing as More than Words on a Page: Using Computers and Multimedia

Chapter 8

Writing has long been recognized as a flow of words on a page. The products of such word flows have been amusing, persuading, teaching, reassuring, instructing, overwhelming, and inspiring readers for centuries. While there are many indications that writing will continue to move readers to think, feel, and act in these and a multitude of other ways for centuries to come, definitions of writing are expanding in the lives of our students, as the Media Awareness Network notes in the quote above. Computers and multimedia open up possibilities for formatting writing that are not possible with a pen and paper. Word processors and the visual images, ideas, and sounds that are available through the Internet, together with software for designing and drawing, as well as digital cameras and video cameras, make it possible to create compositions that are more than words on a page.

In this book, I define *writing* as compositions made up of symbols that communicate meaning to others for particular purposes. A piece of writing could take the form of a multi-paragraph essay. Yet, posters and illustrated stories are also written compositions, as are weblogs, wikis, and PowerPoint presentations, which might contain music and video clips. The decisions that students make about which Internet images to include to illustrate their stories and about which sounds, music, or video clips to use in their PowerPoint presentations, as well as about how to format a brochure or poster, have the same intent as decisions that writers have been making throughout the centuries: to communicate something to someone else. Writers think about which symbols (written and spoken words, graphics, moving images, and sounds) to use and how to put them together to achieve their purpose.

In this chapter, I present ideas for teaching writing using multimedia and digital technology across the curriculum. I offer a wide range of ideas to support teachers who are taking initial steps toward bringing technology into their classrooms and teachers who are already seasoned technology users.

PEN PALS

Students can communicate through email to peers around the world using Internet pen pal programs. Pen pals have provided an authentic audience for children's writing throughout the years. The pen pal letters of today are delivered with a click on the Send button, so the chances of getting a quick response are much greater than they were when pen pals relied on the post office to deliver letters across large expanses of land and sea. Regardless of how the letters are delivered, students take great delight in getting a response to their letters from someone in another province, state, or country. Students want to make a good impression so that their pen pals will write back to them; they are highly motivated to spend time composing and editing so their pen pals can read and understand their email letters.

I recommend two web sites that have made it very easy for teachers to connect with other teachers who wish to match their students with pen pals:

1. Intercultural Email Classroom Connections (IECC) <www.iecc.org>, which is a free service to help teachers link their students with pen pals in other countries. Since its creation in 1992 by three professors from St. Olaf College in Northfield, Minnesota, IECC has distributed over 28 000 requests for email partnerships. Teachers can browse the website to find a class, post a message requesting a class from a particular country, or subscribe to mailing lists containing names of other teachers wishing to find pen pal matches for their students.

2. PALS <www.epalscom>, which is very easy to use. The home page has a search feature through which teachers can write the name of the country from which they would like to find a matching class. Once teachers have found a suitable class, they send an eCard to contact the teacher, and the correspondence begins. Teachers can also register their own classes by writing a paragraph about their class and their reasons for wanting to correspond with another class. Many teachers from countries where English is not the first language write that they want their students to learn and practise their English by corresponding with English-speaking students. They fill out a form giving the number of students in the class, the students' ages, the name of their school and the city and country in which they live, special features of their class, and any means of communicating other than through ePALS messaging. The website claims to have over 133 000 classrooms registered from around the world.

The problems that have always plagued pen pals do not go away with email pen pals. Being matched with a pen pal who never writes back can still be a source of great disappointment for students. However, teachers can make it easier for students to be reliable email pen pals by setting up timelines and providing in-class time to write back to their pen pals. Teachers might also consider whether it is necessary to monitor students' writing to ensure that the content is appropriate before students send the letters to their pen pals. Some teachers ask students to send their emails to the teacher's email account; the teacher then forwards all the emails to the partner teacher. Student confidentiality may be an issue in some schools. If this is the case, students may choose to use pseudonyms and send their emails through their teachers' email accounts.

DIGITAL STORYTELLING

Students have been illustrating their stories, poems, and informational text with drawings and pasted-on photographs or magazine pictures for many years. Digital technology has made elaborate illustrations posssible—students can download graphics from the Internet and can use photographs that they have taken with digital cameras or their cell phones. Students can also scan in their drawings and images from print sources using a scanner. Although the images have been created by someone else, students learn to develop artistic skills when they crop and position the visual images to create the desired effect.

Issues of plagiarism come into play when students download (or anyone downloads) Internet images. Flickr.com is a website for uploading photographs for personal storage, or for sharing with others in the Creative Commons. The person who uploaded the photos indicates whether others can copy and display the photographs or if others may modify the photographs, and whether it is necessary to credit the photographer. The photographs are tagged by the photographer, so students can find images related to the topics of their writing. Wikipedia images are free to those who wish to use them in their own documents through the Wikimedia Commons repository. Contributors give their work freely to this repository with the understanding that anyone can copy, use, and modify any files as long as the source and the authors are credited. The Wikimedia Commons database itself is licensed under the GNU Free Documentation License. Other sources of free graphics are PowerPoint and Microsoft Word (found through the Insert menu).

Students who wish to create stories, poems, or informational pieces that have photographs as their base can download Microsoft Photo Story 3, which is free. Found at <http://www.microsoft.com/windowsxp/using/digitalphotography/photostory/default.mspx>, this software allows students to create slide shows using their own digital photos. They can easily touch up, crop, or rotate pictures, and they can add titles and captions. Students may also add special effects, soundtracks, and their own voice narration to their photo texts. When assessing these texts, teachers may place greater weight on criteria such as "choosing appropriate media that further the writer's purpose" and "putting graphics, sound, and text together in ways that achieve the writer's purpose" because at least as much of the students' creative energies will go into selecting and cropping, rotating, touching up the photographs, and then choosing the appropriate soundtracks and special effects, as will go into writing the captions and the text that they narrate.

POWERPOINT PRESENTATIONS

The art of creating an effective PowerPoint presentation lies in one's ability to summarize ideas concisely and clearly. Like poetry, PowerPoint slides are most effective when they say a lot using only a few words. Cluttered PowerPoint slides are difficult to read and therefore often do not hold an audience's attention. I have geared the activities in chapter 5 on poetry writing toward paring down chunks of text to the most relevant ideas and toward creating outlines; these same suggestions are helpful to students who wish to convey information using PowerPoint slides. Poetry-writing activities, such as creating a list poem on an overhead transparency strips (see page 35) and distilling poems from paragraphs (see page 36) also reinforce the succinct writing needed to create PowerPoint slides.

Designing the slides can take as much time and creative energy as determining the content. Decision making starts with the selection of the background design and colour schemes, the slide layout, the typeface, and possible animation schemes. Students can also add objects, such as digital photographs, scanned images, clip art, or tables from Microsoft Word documents. They can insert movie or sound clips that they have recorded or uploaded from a repository, or they can determine when to have a CD track playing during the presentation. As with the digital stories, when assessing the students' work, it is important that you recognize these decisions as integral to the overall quality of the PowerPoint presentation.

EXPLORING IDEAS BY USING WEBLOGS

Weblogs are online records of a blogger's thoughts, opinions, and experiences that can be updated by the blogger at any time. Each new record is called a *post*. Bloggers can invite comments and additional information from readers at their discretion. Some bloggers use their blogs as online diaries, posting personal information that in the past would have been locked away inside the pages of a pen-and-paper diary. Bloggers who write private thoughts often use pseudonyms to maintain their anonymity. Journalists, academics, and many others use blogs to write commentaries on topics such as political, economic, and cultural events, on literature and sports, and about scientific discoveries. The *Maclean's* magazine website, for example, has links to its columnists' blogs <http://www.macleans.ca/blogs/index.jsp>. The language is less formal and the tone far more conversational (sometimes even cheeky) than those in the magazine itself. The journalist's ponderings are often followed by comments and reactions from readers who applaud or upbraid the journalist bloggers for the positions they take.

In content area classes, students are introduced to provocative and challenging new ideas. Gaining a deeper understanding of these ideas often requires that they mull over the ideas independently and/or bounce the ideas back and forth in conversations with others to gain from their understandings, perspectives, and experiences. Blogs are useful for both private pondering and conversations with others.

Teachers might ask students to respond to a science experiment or to something they have read in a health textbook on either a class blog or a personal blog. As students have done in learning logs with pen and paper in the past, today's students can write their thoughts, questions, and personal connections to the concepts they have encountered through the concrete experience or through their reading in a blog. Other students and the teacher could then add comments and questions to the blog that reinforce and extend the blogger's ideas. The blog creates a window into students' thinking, serving as an informal assessment tool for teachers. The blog also creates a forum in which students can discuss their understandings with peers, their teachers, or with any others who navigate the Internet. Blogs may also be used to extend a discussion that starts in class when teachers assign small-group work. Students can continue the discussion at any time when they are online. The private and conversational writing helps students refine and consolidate their classroom learning.

Bloggers do not have to know hypertext markup language (HTML) in order to post. They simply type what they want to say and follow the easy directions to publish their writing to the blog website. To set up a class blog, check out these two free ones:

1. WordPress.com <www.WordPress.com>, which offers free blogging with either public-access or private blogs and which only members can access. Signing up takes less than five minutes and involves creating a user name and a password. WordPress.com allows you to categorize your posts and automatically create archives based on your categories. Bloggers can choose from over 60 themed backgrounds. WordPress.com has a spell-checker and a preview feature that shows bloggers what their posts will look like before they are published on the blog website. Basic blogging is free of charge with up to 35 users per private blog, but extra space for uploading photographs and videos requires payment for an upgrade of the service.

2. Blogger.com <https://www.blogger.com>, which is also free. It advertises three easy steps to setting up a blog: create an account, name your blog, choose a template. Google owns this service, having purchased it from the original developers in 2002. The service is completely free; there is no mention of any fees, even for uploading photographs and videos. There is no information about the possibility of setting up a private blog that only members can access. Bloggers may write in a number of languages.

COLLABORATIVE WRITING USING WIKIS

Wiki, the Hawaiian word for *fast*, is the name given to a website with pages to which anyone can contribute. Wikis do not require a sophisticated knowledge of computer language, so all contributors can easily write, revise, and edit the content. Students' contributions may be entirely print based or may include visuals, music, sounds, links to websites, and videos. Every change made to a wiki page is tracked and recorded, so that if the content is unacceptable to the wiki's moderator (usually the teacher for classroom wikis), the moderator can remove the content and the page will revert back to a previous version.

Students learn with and from each other when they collaboratively write on wikis that their teachers have set up. Students might create a class newspaper on a wiki. They might write a script for a play that they later perform live for others in their school and then digitally record to upload to the school website. Students in grades 6 or 7 might write poems about life in middle school or junior high school. The poems could be uploaded to the school website, together with photographs or illustrations, to prepare younger students who are entering their first year of middle or junior high school. Not all writing projects lend themselves to collaborative writing, but those that do can be facilitated by creating wikis that allow students to contribute at school and at home. Creating a text collaboratively inspires ideas that students might not have come up with while working alone. All students are responsible for the final product, so students who are more competent with spelling, grammar, and punctuation will have a strong stake in helping fellow contributors with their mechanics. For those students who feel isolated when they write on their own, wikis provide the needed sense of community. For assignments in which students seek out information and take notes, the wiki serves as a storage site for the information that is accessible to all group members. There is no need to email drafts back and forth among group members, since everyone can see the up-to-date draft at the same time.

However, the issues that arise in any cooperative learning activity are at play with collaborative writing on wikis. Assessment of the final product generally takes the form of a group grade. Everyone who participates in the creation of the stories, poems, or informational text on a wiki is given credit for the final product, regardless of the nature or size of their contributions. Although wikis are viewed by educators like Lankshear and Knobel (2006) as more democratic because all participants have a chance to contribute to the best of their abilities and feel successful, wikis do not satisfy students who feel a strong sense of individual ownership of texts they have created. Teachers may need to help wiki groups determine a division of labour that is fair to all students to ensure that everyone makes a meaningful contribution. As well, students can provide a self-assessment of their contributions to ensure greater individual accountability.

Wetpaint.com <www.wetpaint.com> provides free wiki websites that cater to educators. The websites have pop-up ads to pay for the work required to maintain the wiki service, but educators can ask to have an ad-free wiki website. To set up a wiki site, teachers need to create a name, an URL, describe what the wiki will be about, and click on the education category from a menu of categories. They click on buttons to indicate that there will be restricted access and add the names of the participants. To request an ad-free site, teachers simply need to send an email to <education@wetpaint.com> with their school name and address, the wiki's URL, and a short description of how their class will be using the wiki. Within 48 hours, a decision will be made about whether Wetpaint.com will disable the ads.

Contributing to the wiki involves clicking on the EasyEdit button to activate an editing toolbar and then beginning to write or upload photographs, tables, and videos. Wetpaint.com provides support in the form of answers to frequently asked questions to carry out all the activities involved in wiki participation: adding, moving, deleting, and organizing new pages, adding members to the site, sending messages to wiki participants, and adding keyword tags. The website also instructs the teacher on the role of the moderator.

WHY USE COMPUTERS AND MULTIMEDIA TO TEACH WRITING?

From many directions teachers hear the cry to bring new literacies into classrooms. Donna Alvermann (2004), for example, writes that these "are the literacies that adolescents need presently as citizens of a fast-changing world filled with numerous complexities and challenges not yet comprehended" and that "it is easy to imagine a widening gap between youth who have ready access to digital technologies and those who must struggle to get a foot in the door" (p. viii). The Media Awareness Network (2005) found that over half the 5000 young people in Canada between the ages of 11 and 17 that they surveyed in 2003 were spending part of their non-school time each day on the Internet. These young people were looking up information about topics of personal interest, playing games, chatting with friends through instant messaging or email, writing in weblogs or on their personal websites, downloading music, or doing homework. Similarly, in the National School Boards Association 2007 survey of 1300 American 9 to 17 year olds, 96 percent of students with online access used the social networking technologies identified in the Canadian study, adding that they visit online communities such as Facebook, MySpace, and Webkinz. Half these students said they talked about school work in their online socializing.

Teachers have long recognized that bridging the content and skills of the classroom curriculum with students' out-of-school interests helps to make school learning relevant and engaging for students. If young people are interested in and knowledgeable about the Internet, the argument goes, then teachers should build on these interests and experiences when teaching curriculum concepts and skills.

In addition to creating a bridge between students' home and school lives, computers make writing easier. Revision and editing can be done by clicking a mouse and inserting words, images, or sounds; by highlighting and deleting or by cutting and pasting. Research shows that students tend to write longer pieces and revise more frequently when they use a word processor than when they use pen and paper (Goldberg, Russell, and Cook 2003).

Apart from the logistical issues of access to functioning computers and the need for professional development for teachers to feel comfortable in using them, there are few reasons not to teach the use of computers and multimedia.

WORKS CITED

Alvermann, D. Preface. D. Alvermann (ed.). *Adolescents and Literacies in a Digital World*, vii–xi. New York: Peter Lang, 2004.

Goldberg, A., M. Russell, and A. Cook. "The Effect of Computers on Student Writing: A Metaanalysis of Studies from 1992 to 2000." *The Journal of Technology, Learning, and Assessment* 2.1 (2003), 1–52.

Lankshear, C., and M. Knobel. *New Literacies: Everyday Practices and Classroom Learning*, 2nd ed. Maidenhead, Berkshire: McGraw Hill Open University Press, 2006..

National School Boards Association. *Creating and Connecting: Research and Guidelines on Online Social and Educational Networking.* Found 8 February 2008 at <http://www.nsba.org/site/docs/41400/41340.pdf>. Alexandria, VA: Author, 2008.

Media Awareness Network. *Young Canadians in a Wired World: Phase II—Trends and Recommendations.* Ottawa, ON: Author. Found 1 June 2007 at <http://www.media-awareness.ca/english/research/YCWW/phaseII/trends_recommendations.cfm>.

Providing Feedback in Conferences and Assessing Students' Writing — Chapter 9

COMMENTS AND GRADES

As Katherine Paterson relates in the quote above, our student writers enjoy getting feedback from readers. They learn about the power of writing by finding out what readers learned, what they got caught up in, and what they found humorous. They discover more about the intricacies of composing by listening to suggestions for revising or editing particular aspects of their writing. By writing and receiving feedback, students can gain a sense of how well their readers have understood a concept in a particular content area.

As teachers, we spend a lot of time writing comments to students when assessing their writing. We devote sizeable amounts of time to meeting with students, either informally or in pre-arranged student-teacher conferences, to talk about their writing. We hope that our feedback helps them become better at using writing to learn, instruct, entertain, build relationships, direct others' behaviour, or discover more about themselves and their world. We also hope that our comments help students gain confidence as writers. As well, we want our students to be able to use writing and other communication tools to participate in their classes and in other environments.

One other method of providing feedback is by giving grades. This method is controversial but increasingly unavoidable. Many of us are required to provide grades to report on our students' progress. Besides, we often find that our students want a quantitative assessment of the quality of their writing. And so we spend time deliberating about whether to assign an *A* or a *B* to a piece of writing. Yet, we know that these grades are not likely to have a significant effect on students' development as writers. Although they give students a sense of how their writing compares to a particular standard, grades reduce our impressions and analyses of the writing to a simple letter or number. For example, the grade on its own does not inform students that their writing is engaging or thought-provoking. The grade does not provide information about how readily we were able to pick up on the writer's main idea. Nor can it even hint at how we enjoyed the words and expressions or how the writing gave us a sense of the writer's voice. Because grades are increasingly a non-negotiable form of feedback about students' writing, we are constantly searching for methods to grade students' writing and, at the same time, provide more helpful feedback. In this chapter, I present suggestions for scheduling and carrying out student-teacher conferences and for assessing students' narrative, non-narrative, and poetry writing in content areas. I then discuss research-based recommendations for providing written comments on student writing and for helping students make the most of peer feedback.

TIME ISSUES

Making Time for Conferencing

Before students submit their writing for grades, they should receive some feedback from you. This could take the form of a few comments provided on the spot while they write. Or it could take the form of a conversation with students in scheduled student-teacher conferences. It could also come in written form as you write your impressions on works in progress that students hand in to you before the due dates. To become better writers and to gain a deeper understanding of content area concepts, students need an indication of how well their writing fulfills the intended purpose and to what degree they are understanding the concepts from the subject area.

Scheduling time for feedback is often a problem. Some students finish a piece of writing in the first week and will be looking for guidance in revising their writing. Others plan and gather ideas and information for the first few weeks and get started on their writing in the third or fourth week. They need help getting started and envisioning a direction for their writing. If you are a generalist teacher and have 25 or more students in your class, you probably will not be able to have more than one scheduled student-teacher conference with each student during a month. Do not despair. It is not necessary to read and respond to every student's writing every week. I recommend no more than two 10-minute student conferences during a 30- or 40-minute class and do not suggest having conferences during every writing class. Take time while students write independently to schedule on-the-spot feedback. Your scheduled conferences should take place after students are well along in their writing, so that you and the student will have something substantive to talk about. If you teach only content area courses and do not have time for scheduled conferences, you can still give on-the-spot feedback. You can also ask students to hand in their writing at certain points during a six-week unit or whenever they feel they need some feedback. Your written feedback will be particularly helpful if you can also talk to students for a couple of minutes about what you have written.

Working Within Reporting Periods

Three or four times each year, you are likely required to gather assessment information about students' learning and convert it into a number or letter grade for report cards. If you want to be fair to students and base your grades on as much information as possible, you should look at many samples of students' work during each reporting cycle. You will need to set a schedule of due dates to allow students adequate time to plan, write, revise, and edit their writing. Establishing a schedule of due dates will be helpful to all students but particularly to those who tend to get mired in the ongoing writing and revision of one piece of writing for many months. My experience shows that these students welcome the imposition of deadlines. If you are a subject-area specialist, you can work with students to set due dates for one to two pieces of sustained writing throughout a six-week unit. Alternatively, you might use a number of samples of quick-response writing (e.g., short answers to questions) and one sustained piece of writing that students will work on throughout the unit.

If you are a generalist who teaches language arts and content areas, you might ask students to complete two or three pieces during each reporting period for content area grades. The students could select either writing that they have done in content area classes or writing that they have chosen personally for their language arts grade.

STUDENT-TEACHER CONFERENCES

Student-teacher conferences are an invaluable aspect of writers workshop. They allow you to gather information about your students as learners and writers. In these short one-on-one settings, students have a chance not only to express what is important to their learning but also to receive instruction focused on their specific needs.

Processes of Student-Teacher Conferences

Conferences are most effective when they take place in a quiet corner of the classroom where you and the student writer can spend uninterrupted time. Make sure that the rest of the class understands that, during conference time, no other students may try to get your attention or interrupt. If students need help, encourage them to ask a writing buddy or to make a note of the question and consult with you later. They can then either continue working to the best of their abilities or read until you are free.

Students should bring their writing and a pen or pencil to the student-teacher conferences. You should bring the student's records of previous conferences and your observations of the student's learning, together with books, magazines, or your own writing to use as examples in a mini-lesson. Sticky notes are also useful in these conferences; they allow students to write short reminders of what decisions have come out of the conference about what the student should do next with her/his writing. The students can stick the notes to the appropriate places in their writing. You can also use sticky notes to record what you and the student talked about. Use the record-keeping sheet provided

Katie Wood Ray (2001) ends her student-teacher conferences by asking her students to tell what they understood she was saying. This tends to elicit more detailed responses from students than simply asking the closed-ended question "Do you understand?" She then tells her students, "This is what I'm going to write down about what we've talked about in our meeting." This allows for a clear understanding of what happened in the conference, and means that the student and teacher understand each other.

in BLM 9.1 or simply put the sticky notes in the file folder that you keep for each student. These notes provide reminders and information for reporting purposes, and they present an ongoing picture of the student's development as a writer and a content area learner. They are also helpful for planning future mini-lessons.

Referring to notes from previous conferences fosters the students' sense of commitment to decisions they make in student-teacher conferences. Consider the following points when determining a process for carrying out the student-teacher conferences:

- Encourage the student to talk about his/her writing. What does he/she want readers to think, feel, and/or learn?

- Ask the student to find the best part of his/her writing and tell you about it.

- Ask the student to talk about what he/she has learned through writing this piece.

- Summarize what you feel he/she is trying to say in the writing.

- Find out what the student wants help with in order to achieve the desired purpose.

Content of Student-Teacher Conferences

Conferencing About Students' Writing Processes

In student-teacher conferences, you ask questions, make observations, and voice your impressions and feelings; in short, you carry on a conversation just as you would about any topic that interests you and an individual student. You will likely balance your need for information about the students' learning with the students' need for feedback and their desire for new challenges in their writing and content area learning. Ask what your students are working on to be better writers. Ask them to show you where the writing communicates what they have learned about the content area topics. Encourage them to try something in their writing that they have not tried before. Teachers might also consider how students adapt their writing processes to meet the demands of the situation. For example, when writing a persuasive argument for a debate on a school-related issue that will be videotaped and put up on the school website, students would likely spend more time planning, seeking out, and organizing information than they would if they were writing a story about something humorous that happened to them the year before. They also might spend more time revising to cut unnecessary words because the video clip might have time restrictions, whereas the story, as a story, has no parameters on its length. The chart on page 69 lists some questions you might ask to find out more about your students' writing processes.

Conferencing About Students' Writing

During student-teacher conferences, it is important that you talk not just about the students' writing processes but also about the actual writing. Giving positive feedback is immensely important, as it has a significant effect on

QUESTIONS TO HELP ASSESS STUDENTS' WRITING PROCESSES

1. What is the writer's purpose or intention for the writing?

2. What does the writer use to gather information for her/his writing?

3. Why did the writer choose this particular genre?

4. How strong a sense does the writer have of what the genre can do to serve his/her purpose?

5. What does the writer use to organize his/her writing (e.g., webs, lists, table of contents, headings)?

6. What does the writer do to incorporate the content area information (e.g., think about it before considering genre or topic, add it in at the end, weave it in throughout)?

7. What strategies does the writer use to revise (e.g., reread, ask herself/himself questions about what makes sense)?

8. Whom does the writer use as a resource person for revising and editing?

your students' confidence as writers. Make sure to point out the parts that are interesting, entertaining, thought-provoking, and emotion-evoking, in your students' writing, and that your comments are genuine. You should also identify the content area concepts that the student has clearly understood and the elements of writing (e.g., style, organization, conventions) that the student has used successfully.

When making decisions about which elements of the writing or the content area concepts to discuss, consider the following questions:

- What elements of writing or of the content area does the student need help with that will likely not have come up in whole-class instruction?

- Is there something in the student's writing that indicates that I need to teach a concept again?

- What does the student feel he/she needs help with?

You will be able to address only one or two elements of the writing or the content area knowledge in any one conference.

ASSESSING STUDENTS' CONTENT AREA WRITING USING CHECKLISTS

If you are a content area specialist, your emphasis when assessing students' writing will be on their demonstration of their understanding of the content area concepts. You will also be concerned about the effectiveness of their writing in communicating the ideas, but the grade you assign for the written work will primarily reflect the student's conceptual learning. If you teach both content areas and writing, your assessment will likely be balanced between content knowledge and demonstrations of writing competence.

I believe that students must be made aware of the scoring criteria before they begin writing. So that they can focus their learning and their efforts, students need to know what you consider important in each writing assignment. Letting students know how they will be evaluated gives them a sense of their audience.

Whenever I feel it is appropriate, I invite students to help me put together checklists for assessing their writing. I learn a lot about what students know about writing through the criteria they suggest for the checklists. More important, my students have a shared sense of ownership over the assessment process. Most often, students are highly motivated to meet the expectations outlined in the checklists they have helped create. If our students are creating PowerPoint presentations, weblogs, photo essays, websites, digital books, and other non-paper-and-pencil compositions as classroom assignments, we need to find assessment tools that consider students' decision-making skills and how they communicate ideas using print and visual images.

We do not need to discard the writing assessment practices and tools currently in use. Portfolios of student writing, observation checklists, and student-teacher conferences can be opened up to a broader view of students as writers and social beings who use print, digital technologies, and multimedia to communicate with others. For example, assessment criteria might include:

- the choice of media and how the writer or designer uses the media to further her/his purpose.
- a design that highlights the ideas and perspectives being communicated
- students' flexibility in using conventions appropriate to the social context
- an organizational frame that helps writers achieve the desired purpose for the writing

BLMs 9.2, 9.3, 9.4, and 9.5 contain assessment checklists for poetry, narrative, and non-narrative writing, and one that can be used for any type of content area writing. The category *Conventions* runs across all genres. The goal within this category is that students know the standard conventions for communicating clearly. Another criterion that runs across genres is students' effective integration of content area information in a manner that is appropriate for the genre and the audience. Appendix A contains examples showing how teachers have used the checklists to assess particular students' writing.

THE ROLE OF SELF-ASSESSMENT

Viewing self-assessment as a learning tool, I used to ask my elementary and university students to assign a grade, and then I averaged their grade with the grade that I had assigned. It did not work very well, though, because students gave themselves a grade that reflected their personality and their needs to a greater degree than it reflected the effectiveness of their writing. Students who were self-effacing gave themselves lower grades than those who needed a good grade to boost their grade point average or those who were extremely self-confident. My students told me that they felt very uncomfortable assigning grades to their own writing. Although I still believe in the importance of self-assessment, I no longer put students through that agony. Now I ask students to write comments explaining what they wanted to achieve in their writing and how well they felt they achieved their intentions. These written assessments are invaluable to me when I assess the writing. They give me a strong sense of what the students have learned about both

WRITING PROCESSES AND GOALS: SELF-ASSESSMENT

1. What are you hoping that readers will learn, think, or feel after reading or viewing your assignment? What parts of your assignment do you feel work best to help readers learn, think, or feel this?

2. What did you spend most of your time doing on this assignment? Why was this the most time-consuming thing you did? How did it improve your assignment so it achieves your purpose?

3. What did you do in this assignment that you haven't done before or that you usually don't do on your assignments? How did it make your assignment better so it achieves your purpose?

4. What did you learn about writing and about your writing processes through doing this assignment?

their writing and the content area concepts. If students provided information about specific qualities of writing that they were working on and either still struggled with or were successful in mastering, I feel they demonstrated a lot of learning. If they made unsupported assessments using words from the scoring guides in general ways, I feel they demonstrated either a need to learn more about the qualities of writing, or a need to learn how to attend to the nuances of their writing and writing processes. A self-assessment such as this could also be an indicator that the teacher must do more to demonstrate the value of writing and of self-assessment to motivate the student. I take students' self-assessments to heart and incorporate them into my assessment of their work. The questions in the chart above provide a framework for students' self-assessment.

ISSUES REGARDING TEACHERS' WRITTEN FEEDBACK

Making Comments on Students' Writing: Some Recommendations

There has been a great deal of research on the topic of writing comments on students' writing. While most of the research has been conducted at the post-secondary level, the recommendations that come from this research ring true for grades 4 to 8 teachers, as well. See a list of recommendations below (adapted from Straub 2000). Be aware that they might not all be appropriate for every student. Combine these with your own knowledge of your students and your classroom context. This caution is equally important when making decisions about how to respond to students' writing.

RECOMMENDATIONS FOR TEACHERS' WRITTEN FEEDBACK

1. Use a conversational tone, imagining that the student is beside you and you are talking together about the writing.

2. Focus on content, organization, and purpose. Attend to style and conventions to a lesser degree.

3. Focus on two or three concerns in a given set of comments. Students have a better chance of learning the concepts or skills if they have to attend to only a few at any one time.

4. Respond to early drafts in a different manner from the way you do to later drafts. Emphasize focus, content knowledge, and overall organization on the early drafts. Address wording, sentence structure, and writing conventions in later drafts.

Writing Assessment Is Subjective

Much of my research has focused on the ways in which teachers assess and respond to boys' writing and girls' writing. In one study, I looked at the differences in the written feedback that 108 grade-6 teachers gave to girls' writing and to boys' writing. I found that teachers tended to write more comments that corrected and criticized the writing when they thought the writer was a boy. When they thought the writer was a girl, they wrote more open-ended questions (Peterson and Kennedy 2006).

In addition, I asked approximately 200 teachers in grades 3, 6, 8, and 9 to read student writing and identify characteristics of the writing that pointed to the writer's gender (Peterson 1998). They identified writers as girls when they felt the writing was detailed, well organized, and had strong, specific vocabulary and character development, and used writing conventions well. They assessed the writing very differently when they identified the writers as boys, describing the writing as short, lacking in detail and character development, using too-general vocabulary, and lacking in attention to writing conventions well. The teachers were talking about the same pieces of writing. The only things that differed were their perceptions of whether the writer was female or male. These perceptions did not translate into grading patterns that favoured girls, except in one instance. In this case, teachers who thought that the writer was a girl scored the writing higher in every scoring category than teachers who thought that the writer was a boy. In addition, in one or two cases, the scores that teachers assigned to the writing ranged from a level 1 (below the acceptable standard) to a level 4 (above the acceptable standard). Teachers seemed to have very different ideas about what constituted good writing.

I present these results as a reminder that assessing writing is a subjective process. I do not believe we should see this as a weakness, however. Making personal meaning and bringing in background experiences, perspectives, and values are natural to any reading experience. What is important is that we reflect on our experiences and values and become aware of how they can influence our assessments of students' writing.

Recognizing the social nature of writing means that we also have to view ourselves—that is, the teachers who assess students' writing—as social beings. Our beliefs, values, and experiences influence how we read and assess students' writing. We are not able to be completely objective in our assessment if we attempt to suppress or ignore the perspectives and experiences that make us who we are. Instead, we need to consider how our expectations and values bring some features of student writing to the foreground and how they shine a less favourable light on particular features when we assess student writing. One thing we could do to this end is enter into dialogue with other teachers about what constitutes good writing within various contexts. We might also assess students' writing collaboratively with colleagues, frequently discussing our responses to particular pieces of writing to gain new perspectives on the writing.

ISSUES REGARDING STUDENTS' FEEDBACK

What Peers Can Offer

When they receive peer feedback, students are in a position to gain a strong sense of audience and to experience a wide range of ideas and perspectives. Some researchers claim that peer feedback is more genuine than teacher feedback, because it is not connected to the final assessment of the writing (Gere and Stevens 1985). In my research in a grade-8 class, I observed that four types of peer feedback strongly influenced students' drafting and the revisions of their writing:

1. The writer and her/his peers played with ideas for the writing.
2. Peers asked for clarification.
3. Peers showed emotional responses to the writing.
4. Peers questioned the plausibility of particular ideas or events.

As they wrote, the students in the classes I was using for research asked questions of the peers sitting close to them and tossed out ideas for deliberation. They seemed to use this talking to explore ideas. Although peers' indications of where the writing was unclear led to some revisions, feedback that questioned the plausibility and showed emotional response was particularly powerful in shaping the writing. The students were concerned about appearing foolish or incompetent in terms of their knowledge of the world and of what was acceptable within the classroom social network. Students were saved potential embarrassment by having an opportunity to negotiate the social meanings within a less threatening small-group setting before reading their writing to the whole class in authors chair.

Establishing Routines for Peer Feedback: Some Recommendations

Authors chair and authors group—two activities that are often included in the writers workshop structure—provide opportunities for peer feedback. In these settings, some students flourish and others do not, often depending on their confidence and competence as writers and their social popularity in the classroom.

Authors chair, for example, provides an ideal audience for students' writing. I have observed many students delighting in their classmates' attention and acclaim for their writing. I also know some students who reluctantly complete a piece of writing or write something safe that they know peers will accept in order to avoid embarrassment during authors chair. Some students, such as those in the research conducted by Timothy Lensmire (1994) and by Pam Gilbert (1993), used their writing to try to hurt other students and assert their social status in the classroom. In these studies, socially powerful students included characters in their narratives that resembled particular classmates. These characters were humiliated in ways that embarrassed the peers they represented. I am rethinking the use of authors chair because of this research and my own observations in classrooms.

Authors chair does not have to be a class-wide performance of students' writing. Instead, they might conduct readings of their writing to small groups of trusted classmates, or they could read to small groups of students in younger grades. Students might also record audio or video versions of their writing and have the tapes available for peers to listen to or view in the classroom library. Students might read selected parts of their writing, skipping the parts that they wish to keep private. Students should not be required to read every piece of their writing to the class. A good rule of thumb is to allow students choices about their audiences. Participating in a whole-class authors chair should not be the only option.

There are reasons for my rethinking of the practice of author groups. Donald Graves (1994, p. 133) observes that

> children ask questions before they have thought long enough to understand the text, and most of their questions are of the *pro forma* type: "What's your favourite part? What will you write next?" It is almost as if the children have adopted formulaic questions irrespective of the actual piece the author is sharing.

Not only can some students feel uncomfortable about giving and receiving feedback from peers, but also the usefulness of the feedback can be limited if students in a particular group are not committed to helping their fellow writers.

In a previous book (Peterson 2003), I recommend bringing together groups of three or four students in an authors group to read their drafts to each other and take turns describing effective features and what was unclear or confusing. Since writing that book, I have had more opportunities to observe students while they are giving and receiving feedback. My observations have shown that the most valuable peer feedback is given in two settings: (1) spontaneously, while students are writing, and (2) when a teacher sets aside time for students to exchange their writing with a partner of their choosing. In these settings, the teacher gives the students general questions to get them started talking about each other's writing. These questions include: What did you get out of the piece? What stands out about the piece? What questions does the writing raise for you? One teacher I know demonstrated how writers need genuine feedback on the clarity, plausibility, and engagement of their writing. He established how to work with peers to show respect and applaud writers who try new things. These types of practices helped students get useful feedback from peers while the complexities of social relationships within classrooms remained respectful.

Teachers might consider how peers respond to the students' writing, how students expect peers to respond, and what they do to ensure this response. Teachers might enter into conversations with groups of students about what they expect girls and boys of their age to write about and what kinds of words, actions, phrases, topics, characters, and settings they enjoy writing and reading about. Teachers might extend this by looking at examples that sit outside the gender parameters in an effort to broaden students' perspectives on acceptable social meanings that can be communicated in their writing.

In student-teacher conferences or when providing written feedback to students, teachers need to ask students about their processes in terms of the demands of the writing context in student-teacher conferences. They also need to observe what students are doing to plan, write, revise, and edit.

WORKS CITED

Gere, A.R., and R.S. Stevens. "The Language of Writing Groups: How Oral Response Shapes Revision." In S.W. Freedman (ed.), *The Acquisition of Written Language: Response and Revision,* 85–105. Norwood, NJ: Ablex, 1985.

Gilbert, P. "A Story that Couldn't be Read." In P. Gilbert (ed.), *Gender Stories and the Language Classroom,* 11–36. Victoria, Australia: Deakin University Press, 1993.

Graves, D. *A Fresh Perspective on Writing.* Portsmouth, NH: Heinemann, 1994.

Lensmire, T. *When Children Write: Critical Re-Visions of the Writing Workshop.* New York: Teachers College Press, 1994.

Paterson, K. *A Sense of Wonder: On Reading and Writing Books for Children.* New York: Plume, 1995.

Peterson, S. "Evaluation and Teachers' Perceptions of Gender in Sixth-Grade Student Writing." *Research in the Teaching of English* 33.2 (1998), 181–208.

_____. *Guided Writing Instruction: Strategies to Help Students Become Better Writers.* Winnipeg: Portage & Main Press, 2003.

Peterson, S., and K. Kennedy. "Grade-Six Teachers' Feedback on Girls' and Boys' Narrative and Persuasive Writing." *Written Communication* 23.1 (2006), 36–62.

Straub, R. "The Student, the Text, and the Classroom Context: A Case Study of Teacher Response. *Assessing Writing* 7.1 (2000), 23–55.

Wood Ray, K. *The Writing Workshop: Working through the Hard Parts (and They're All Hard Parts).* Urbana, IL: NCTE, 2001.

Supporting Struggling Writers

Chapter **10**

FINDING IDEAS AND BUILDING A KNOWLEDGE BASE FOR WRITERS

Stephen Leacock (above) was rather cavalier about difficulties that writers encounter. Some of the students in our classes might say that it was easy for him to be clever about what makes writing difficult—he wrote countless books and has a humour award named after him. They would not disagree that seeking out ideas is onerous, however. It is just that their list of writing difficulties does not end there. Our struggling writers often worry about producing something of interest to readers. Some students may be learning English as a second or third language in addition to learning to write. Others may be afraid to write what is important to them for fear of peer ridicule. Some of our struggling writers labour with the physical act of moving a pen along a page. These students tend not to take time to plan their ideas and organize their thoughts when given a writing task. They toil with the forms and conventions of writing.

These students often try to avoid writing and struggle with it throughout their school years. Finding ways to support our struggling writers involves considering both their cognitive needs and their social needs. Helping students find ideas for their writing and modelling ways to develop characters and punctuate sentences correctly go a long way in nurturing our students' writing development. We must also think about the social environment in which our students are writing. This involves showing students how important writing is in their lives and sending constant messages about how important writing is to us. It also involves aligning the purposes for writing closely with those beyond the school. Another consideration is the effect of writing on students' social relationships within the classroom, especially when they are sharing their work. To begin this chapter, I suggest ways to support students' writing development. Next, I suggest ways to support students as social beings who navigate the complexities of social lives within and beyond our classrooms.

In content area classes, finding ideas for writing is not a problem—the content area concepts set parameters on the topics. Yet, if students are to generate ideas to write on content area topics, they still need to draw from a deep well of information and experiences. Reading, interviewing, observing, experimenting, and surveying are the best ways to fill that well.

After students have started writing, encourage them to continue to gather information by reading, interviewing, observing, experimenting, and surveying. Gathering information does not take place only at the beginning of a writing project. The initial planning and note taking rarely provide all the information needed to complete an essay, poem, or story on a content area subject. I find in my own writing experience that after a while it becomes evident that there are gaps in what I know about the topic. I have to seek out further information to answer new questions that have come up while writing. Student writers in your content area classes will likely find similar needs as they write. When they are stuck for ideas, they may find it helpful to seek out information on the Internet, in books or magazines, or by interviewing someone in the school or someone who lives and works outside the school. Struggling writers may need support in identifying and organizing the information they need (see chapter 3 for some helpful mini-lessons). When we teach writing in content area classes, we can pick up on students' unsuccessful attempts to make sense of a topic in the first drafts of their writing rather than at the end of a unit when students hand in an exam. Students' writing is a mirror of their understanding (or misunderstanding) of a topic. This is clearly demonstrated in the following sentence, written by a college student: "Actually, the fall of empires has been a good thing, because it gives more people a chance to exploit their own people without outside interference" (Henriksson 2001, p. 130). Likely to generate a few chuckles, this sentence also signals the student's struggles to understand the concepts. By monitoring student writing at all stages, we can catch these kinds of misunderstandings early on and help clarify concepts. Conferencing with students provides both the opportunity to clarify inaccurate understandings of concepts and support for students' writing development.

DIFFICULTIES WITH THE CONVENTIONS OF WRITING

For the most part, students' struggles with spelling, punctuation, grammar, and the specific forms of various genres arise from a lack of familiarity with conventions. Often, these students find that what they intended to write is not what ended up on the page. These students benefit from reading through their writing with a more competent person, who can help to identify the errors. It is also helpful to give explicit instruction, together with repeated exposure in their reading and opportunities to try out what they are learning about conventions in their own writing.

Have your students practise using the conventions by writing and editing their own and others' writing on a daily basis. In chapter 7, I provide a range of suggestions for teaching and reinforcing the correct use of writing conventions. Students who struggle with writing may need reminders to help them apply the conventions in their writing. References might take the form of posters or personal notebooks that have examples of the punctuation, spelling, and grammar generalizations that students learn in mini-lessons. In addition, writing on computers seems to highlight the need for punctuation.

My research on writing assessment shows that many teachers tend to correct every convention error they see in students' writing. This not only takes a huge amount of time but also creates a burden on the struggling writer. Regardless of the colour of the ink, a blanket of corrections laid on a piece of writing overwhelms and often paralyzes struggling writers. Where do they start when it seems that everything has to be redone? I have found that it is best to focus on one or two types of error and to praise students for the writing conventions they have used correctly. If students direct their attention to correcting one or two types of convention errors, there is a much greater likelihood that they will learn the spelling, grammar, or punctuation rules and use them in future writing.

Steve Graham (1990) advises teachers of students with disabilities to guard against putting an overly strong emphasis on mechanics when teaching writing. In his research about students' perceptions of good writing, students with disabilities often perceived that the appearance of the text and the mechanics were more important than the content. I recommend the following practices to help students with learning disabilities focus on what they are writing, rather than on how it looks:

- Invite students to write about topics that are interesting to them and that they want to learn more about.

- Invite students to consider audiences other than their teacher for their writing and then send or give the writing to that intended audience to read.

- Encourage students to take up writing projects that are challenging enough to warrant the effort and time needed to create a quality product and, at the same time, that are not overwhelming.

- Examine the texts that students write outside classrooms (e.g., wikis, blogs, text messages) and show how the message is more important than the form. However, make sure that students recognize that the audience's expectations for adherence to writing conventions are less demanding than those of audiences of more formal writing.

I found in my research that teachers have cited the use of the spell-checker in word processing programs as a reason for discouraging students to compose on computers. Their fear is that students will not learn to spell because the spell checker will take care of their misspellings. Other researchers, however, have shown that spell checkers encourage students to edit for spelling. Charles McArthur, Steve Graham, Jacqueline Haynes, and Susan de La Paz (1996) found that middle-grade students with learning disabilities corrected 9 percent of their spelling errors when they did not use the spell checker in their word-processing program. The number of corrected spelling errors rose to 37 percent when they did use it. Spell checkers have limitations, however. They do not identify words that are spelled correctly but are used incorrectly (e.g., homonyms such as *their* instead of *there*). And, if students' misspellings are not recognizable to

Alice, a grade 5-6 social studies teacher, observed that, when her students edited their writing on computers, they added punctuation, such as quotation marks, more consistently than when they wrote with pen and paper. She felt that the computer screen made it easier for students to see the need for punctuation marks.

the spell checker, the suggestions offered to students will not be helpful. These limitations can be overcome with explicit instruction providing students with strategies for creating spellings that the spell checker will recognize (e.g., type a phonetic spelling). See chapter 7 for some helpful proofreading strategies.

PHYSICAL AND MENTAL EFFORTS REQUIRED

The very challenge of grasping and manipulating a pen or pencil requires some students' full concentration. These struggling students have little energy left for communicating ideas. Graham, Berninger, Abbott, Abbott, and Whitaker (1997) found that many students' difficulties with writing fluency stemmed more from their handwriting problems than from problems with spelling. This does not mean that we should not ask students to carry out any writing tasks until their handwriting improves, however. Instead, use tools such as computers to make the physical task of writing easier. Students are then freed up to think about the messages they want to communicate rather than about how they will form the words. Revision is a laborious exercise when students work with a pen or pencil; it is much quicker and less distracting on a computer. The easy access of the computer screen makes collaboration among students much easier; all members of the collaborative writing team can readily see the work in progress. The final computer-created product generally looks more attractive than a handwritten one and is easier to read, so struggling writers can feel a greater sense of accomplishment with their writing. If students do not have strong keyboarding skills, the effects of computer use on their revisions will be minimized without assistance from peers or teachers. Struggling writers carry out substantive revisions to the content of their writing, for example, when they compose using computers and then meet with a peer who gives feedback on the clarity of the writing, their emotional response to the writing, what they think the writing is trying to achieve, and their suggestions for changes that would make the writing stronger.

Often, students struggle with writing because it requires a great deal of focused attention. Struggling students welcome short writing assignments and often prefer answering questions or writing short paragraphs. We do not need to deny these students the experiences of discovery writing, however. Poetry can provide a focus for students to play with and develop ideas in a short form. (See chapter 5 for suggestions to help writers communicate something important to them about the content area topic through poetry.)

Donald Graves (1994) and I have found the opposite to be true as well. Some students have no trouble sustaining their focus on writing. Instead, they have trouble completing their writing. I observed a grade-6 student who wrote a never-ending horse story. From September through May, she wrote 50 single-spaced typed pages on the same story. One day I dropped the photocopy I had made of her story, and the unnumbered pages scattered all over the floor. I could not put that story back together again. There were many redundancies, and the flow of the story was very hard to follow. The student herself told me that she wished she had had some deadlines for her writing. In the previous year, her teacher had required her to complete a number of pieces of writing each term, and she had finished a number of pieces. A good way to place some boundaries on the time they spend on any one piece is to work with students to set deadlines for their writing. In content area classes, these deadlines often coincide naturally with the end of a unit of study.

PLANNING AND REVISING

Researchers who looked at the writing processes of successful writers found that planning, whether it was written, oral, or in the writer's head, is important to producing good writing. Many writers with learning disabilities minimize the role of planning in their writing processes. They often "go with the flow," allowing each idea that they write to lead into the next idea without thinking about their overall purpose for their writing or their audience's needs.

The Self-Regulated Strategy Development (SRSD) model, developed by Gary Troia, Steve Graham, and Karen Harris (1999) has been used successfully to help students set goals and organize ideas in their writing. There are several features of their model that all teachers can fold into mini-lessons for struggling writers:

- The teacher uses think-alouds while modelling a planning process such as setting goals for writing, brainstorming ideas that could be included in the writing, and voices her/his thoughts about how ideas might flow from one to the next so that readers can readily follow along. The teacher writes so that all students can see, using a computer and an LCD projector, an overhead projector, or the blackboard. While writing, the teacher voices her/his thoughts regarding goal setting, brainstorming, and organizing. The teacher might also carry the writing process further by starting to write, showing how the original plan changes and evolves as the writing progresses. Sometimes the teacher needs to add or delete ideas in order to meet the original purposes and to fit the needs of the intended audience. The teacher provides a rationale for each of the decisions made while setting goals, brainstorming, organizing, and writing and revising.

- Students identify what their teacher did and his/her rationale for each process. They compare and contrast their planning on a recent piece of writing and assess which of the teacher's processes might help them in their next writing project.

- The teacher and students together think of a way to help students remember the processes that students feel would be helpful. They might create a poster with words and/or images describing or showing the process, or they might create a rhyme to help them remember.

- In student-teacher conferences, the teacher talks to students about their writing processes, asking them to identify their planning strategies. This is in addition to talking about the written drafts that students have composed.

- Students conduct a self-assessment of their written products and of their writing processes, identifying the goal setting, audience considerations, organizational strategies, revision strategies, and other writing conventions that they used. They provide a rationale for each process they carried out. Students also consider what they could do, in terms of their processes, to improve their writing the next time.

Repeat the practices identified in the list above numerous times throughout the school year. Brian Wong (2000) found that students with learning disabilities started internalizing the writing processes after many months of teacher modelling and feedback. Without the prolonged attention to teaching writing processes, such instruction has not been very successful in helping struggling writers maintain the strategies.

LEARNING ENGLISH AS AN ADDITIONAL LANGUAGE

Students learning English as an additional language (English language learners, or ELLs) are learning English vocabulary and sentence structure or at the same time as they are learning to write. Although ELLs develop *conversational* fluency fairly quickly, they need much more experience and support in developing English *writing* proficiency. In everyday conversation they often use short, disjointed phrases using a limited number of high-frequency words. Writing places much greater demands on ELLs, because it requires complete sentences, well-organized paragraphs, and specific vocabulary to develop ideas. In addition, it is important to be aware that some classroom writing assignments may be culturally inappropriate for some students and may make them uncomfortable. Monika Smith and Donald Qi (2003) give the example that, in some cultures, children never oppose an older person's opinion because it draws undue attention to the child. Asking such students to compose an opinion piece that counters the opinion of an adult they know places them in a difficult position.

ELLs have learned a great deal about how language works and about the content area concepts when learning to speak and write in their original language. Research has shown that ELLs might use this knowledge by writing in their original tongue and then translating it into English (Kobayashi and Rinnert 1992). Alternatively, they can think of the words they want in their first language and then translate the words when they write them (Qi 1998). Some struggling ELLs may benefit from having bilingual colleagues, parents, outside tutors, or peers who share their language to help them translate. The ELLs write what they can in English and then use their first language to express the rest of what they want to say. Alternatives to writing, such as drawing and labelling or giving oral presentations, are helpful when ELLs are first learning English.

These students should move into more complex writing as quickly as possible, however, because they need to develop writing skills to communicate their learning across the curriculum (Smith and Qi 2003). Some schools are inviting their ELLs to write autobiographies, stories, poems, and informational texts in both their original languages and English. Students compose the texts in their original languages and then translate them into English. The two languages appear side by side or one above the other on a page. Often, parents and other community members are invited into classrooms to help translate the texts from one language to the other. Teachers' and peers' interest in reading these dual-language stories, poems, and informational texts send a clear message to ELLs that they and their languages and cultures are valued. All students gain a greater understanding and appreciation of cultures and perspectives other than their own through reading these dual-language texts. The ELLs feel successful, as they have been able to use a wider vocabulary in their original-language writing than in their English writing. Thornwood Public School and Michael Cranny School are two Ontario schools with websites that explain how teachers set up their classrooms to support their students in writing dual-language books (see <http://thornwood.peelschools.org/Dual/about.htm> and <http://www.multiliteracies.ca/index.php/folio/viewDocument/8/4495>).

When matching ELLs with peers, rather than having the student whose original language is English serve as the helper and the ELL as the helpee, it is a good idea to place both students in helping roles. Both the ELL and her/his peer feel they have something to contribute if the ELL first helps her/his partner in carrying out the assigned task. Then, when the roles are switched and the ELL is being helped, she/he has observed a successful performance of the task and has peer assistance to carry out the task herself/himself. Both students are placed in positions in which their talents and skills are valued.

The teaching suggestions throughout this book use published literature as models for students' writing; they provide many examples for helping ELLs express themselves in writing using the English words, sentence structures, paragraph organizations, and spelling in various contexts. It is helpful, as well, for ELLs to write in a number of genres. By writing and getting feedback from peers and teachers, ELLs can practise and refine what they are learning about using English to communicate their ideas. When assessing ELLs' writing, it is important that we pay attention to the message and content of the writing as well as to the spelling and grammar errors that indicate that the students are still learning English. When following the suggestions I present in chapter 9 for conferencing and assessing writing, try to balance considerations for furthering students' proficiency in learning English as well as their competence in writing and learning concepts.

MOTIVATION TO WRITE

Often, we confuse a lack of motivation for writing with a student's struggle to write. A half-page essay from a student following weeks of class time devoted to writing may not be evidence of the student's struggle with writing. Instead, this may signal a student's resistance to writing or a lack of motivation to write. Research on motivation for writing shows that interest, relevance, and a sense of purpose are critical to engaging students in writing (Pajares and Johnson 1994). My own observations provide yet another example. I was recently in a grade-6 science class. Fifteen minutes into a class devoted to writing, two boys who had been kicked out of class the previous week for misbehaving were sitting together drawing lines on blank paper. As I had observed in the previous class, they were resisting getting started on their writing. I found out that they both loved basketball and had thought about writing a story that would include motion concepts. This had proven to be too difficult; they could not find ideas for a story. I suggested that they write a manual on how to play basketball. One of the boy's eyes lit up as he said, "We could write about playing basketball on Mars!" For the rest of the class time, the two boys wrote furiously. Though they had initially planned to write together, by the end of the 40-minute period, one boy had written two paragraphs of a story and the other had written five tips on playing basketball on Mars. Their enthusiasm for the topic pulled them past their initial resistance to writing.

Assigning open-ended writing projects provides space for students to tap into their interests and knowledge base. You might leave the choice of genre open to students, or you might free students up to write whatever they want on a topic as long as they demonstrate their knowledge of a particular concept. Bringing in the graphics, sound, and video capabilities of the multimedia and digital technologies that students use outside the classroom is likely to enhance their motivation to write. Students might create PowerPoint presentations to demonstrate their learning, for example. They might also use digital video clips or digital pictures and create websites to communicate what they have learned. The media provide other forms of communication that complement what students write. They also provide information and ideas to spur students' own generation of ideas for their writing. Some students may find that using multimedia forms takes their attention away from writing and revising. I have observed students spending whole class periods figuring out the type size and font for the title of their writing, for example. I have also experienced how Internet searching for the right image or the right sound for a multimedia piece can consume hours of my time. Instruction on how to conduct fruitful, efficient searches for information, graphics, and sound and video clips are helpful to all students. Also helpful are reminders to draw on the Internet knowledge and experiences of peers and teachers, and discussions on how to set timelines for carrying out the various processes required to put together a multimedia piece.

Enthusiasm for writing is generated when students use classroom writing for their own social purposes (Blair and Sanford 2004; Dyson 1993; Dyson 2003). Students can build relationships with peers and gain status within the peer social network by, among other things, naming their characters after classmates or by using humour or grotesque details to entertain their peers. The more broadly we define a topic and genre for students, the more space we create for students to achieve the academic goal and, at the same time, commandeer the writing to achieve their own goals.

Tap into students' desire for social participation by providing the option for them to collaborate with peers when they write. I find that having students write in pairs is optimal, since larger groups demand sophisticated social and communication skills that are often beyond their abilities. Invite students to write pieces that they can perform, such as choral speeches, plays, readers theatre, and radio or puppet plays. Students enjoy the favourable attention they get from peers who vie for roles in the performances and who are entertained by the performance. On countless occasions, I have observed delight and satisfaction on students' faces as peers show enjoyment of something they have written and performed. This is infinitely more motivating than writing a paper for a letter grade and a few comments from a teacher. Although I suggest that students weave their social purposes into their classroom writing, I also caution against giving them carte blanche. Sometimes students' social purposes include hurting or otherwise distressing peers. For example, a socially popular grade-3 student in Timothy Lensmire's (1994) study embarrassed a boy who had upset her and humiliated a socially unpopular girl in the class by writing a story in which the boy was the love interest of the socially unpopular girl. This girl's lack of social success was underscored in the story by her desire to grow "zits" to attract boys. In such situations, we cannot be blind to the damage caused when students commandeer their classroom writing for their own social purposes. We need to monitor their writing and place restrictions on content that might embarrass or hurt classmates. Discuss with students the consequences of their writing. Read books and participate in drama activities in class that are designed to develop empathy. These types of activity might help communicate the message that students should be respectful of peers and not use their writing to harm classmates in any way.

Tapping into students' social needs and desires also involves giving boys and girls space to express their masculinity or femininity in their writing. This issue has come to our attention in the past few years because writing test results show that many boys do not develop the writing competencies that most girls do. This disparity might be attributed to boys' resistance to conform to teachers' and test designers' expectations for writing. Often, these expectations favour a more feminine style of writing, which is characterized by lots of description and detail, conformity to writing conventions and organizational structures, and the absence of violence.

In my research (2001; 2002), boys and girls in grades 4 and 8 explained that boys ran the risk of being ridiculed by peers if their writing took on feminine qualities. Because of the more widely respected position of boys' topics, themes, and characters, boys felt that they needed to write in ways that clearly identified them to others in their classroom as masculine. Girls felt that they could write about topics and in styles that were considered feminine or masculine and not suffer ridicule and embarrassment, however. Make every effort to support boys' and girls' social needs by opening up the accepted forms of writing to those preferred by boys and girls respectively. Thomas Newkirk (2002) suggests assignments for writing that:

- have the quick pace of an action movie or cartoon
- contain exaggerations, slapstick humour, absurdities, and sound effects for audience appeal
- show loyalties to popular youth culture

These features might also be incorporated into the checklists for use in assessing students' writing. Often, the writing styles and features that boys have developed to demonstrate their masculinity and develop social relationships within the classroom social network are not recognized in our feedback on their writing.

Peter Daly, Joan Salters, and Catherine Burns (1998) caution that gender stereotypes may be strengthened when students follow their gender preferences exclusively, however. Some teacher intervention is needed to introduce students to a wide range of possibilities for their writing. In Janice White's study (1990), for example, small groups of girls who wrote science fiction and adventure stories for younger boys used domestic themes and wrote about the characters' emotional responses to the exciting situations. Small groups of boys who wrote fantasy stories for younger girls cast female characters in humorous and dangerous positions as tomboys. Typically, boys do not include female protagonists in their writing. Teachers can help persuade both boys and girls to venture away from these stereotypes. Teachers might also introduce literature in which adult writers have crossed gender lines. They can invite discussion about gender stereotypes and the restrictions they place on male and female writers.

WORKS CITED

Blair, H., and K. Sanford. "Morphing Literacy: Boys' Reshaping their School-Based Literacy Practices." *Language Arts* 81.6 (2004), 452–460.

Daly, P., J. Salters, and C. Burns. "Gender and Task Interaction: Instant and Delayed Recall of Three Story Types." *Educational Review* 50.3 (1998), 269–275.

Dyson, A.H. *Social Worlds of Children Learning to Write in an Urban Primary School.* New York: Teachers College Press, 1993.

_____. *The Brothers and Sisters Learn to Write: Popular Literacies in Childhood and School Cultures.* New York: Teachers College Press, 2003.

Graham, S. "The Role of Production Factors in Learning Disabled Students' Compositions." *Journal of Educational Psychology* 82 (1990), 781–791.

Graham, S., V. Berninger, R.D. Abbott, S.P. Abbott, and O. Whitaker. "The Role of Mechanics in the Composing of Elementary School Students: A New Methodological Approach." *Journal of Educational Psychology* 89 (1997), 170–182.

Graves, D. *A Fresh Look At Writing.* Portsmouth, NH: Heinemann, 1994.

Henriksson, A. *Non Campus Mentis: World History According to College Students.* New York: Workman Publishing, 2001.

Kobayashi, S., and C. Rinnert. "Effects of First Language on Second Language Writing: Translation Versus Direct Composition." *Language Learning* 42 (1992), 183–215.

Lensmire, T. *When Children Write: Critical Re-Visions of the Writing Workshop.* New York: Teachers College Press, 1994.

McArthur, C., S. Graham, J. Haynes, and S. de La Paz. "Spelling Checkers and Students with Learning Disabilities: Performance Comparisons and Impact on Spelling." *Journal of Special Education* 30 (1996), 35–57.

Newkirk, T. *Misreading Masculinity: Boys, Literacy and Popular Culture.* Portsmouth, NH: Heinemann, 2002.

Pajares, F.K., and M.J. Johnson. "Confidence and Competence in Writing: The Role of Self-Efficacy, Outcome Expectancy, and Apprehension." *Research in the Teaching of English* 28 (1994), 313–331.

Peterson, S. "Gender Identities and Self-Expression in Classroom Narrative Writing." *Language Arts* 78.5 (2001), 451–457.

_____. "Gender Meanings in Grade-Eight Students' Talk about Classroom Writing." *Gender and Education* 14.4 (2002), 351–366.

Qi, D. S. "An Inquiry into Language-Witching in Second Language Composing Processes." *Canadian Modern Language Review* 54 (1998), 413–435.

Robertson, C. (ed.) *The Dictionary of Quotations.* Hertfordsire, UK: Wordsworth Editions Ltd., 1997.

Smith, M., and D. Qi. "A Complex Tangle: Teaching Writing to ELL Students in the Mainstream Classroom." In S. Peterson (ed.), *Untangling Some Knots in Teaching K-8 Writing*, 52–65. Newark, NJ: International Reading Association, 2003.

Troia, G.A., S. Graham, and K.R. Harris. "Teaching Students with Learning Disabilities to Mindfully Plan when Writing." *Exceptional Children* 65.2 (1999), 235–252.

White, J. "On Literacy and Gender." In R. Carter (ed.), *Knowledge about Languages and the Curriculum*, 181–196. London, UK: Hodden and Stroughton, 1990.

Wong, B.Y.L. "Writing Strategies Instruction for Expository Essays for Adolescents with and without Learning Disabilities." *Topics in Language Disorders* 20.4 (2000), 29–44.

INTEGRATING NARRATIVE WRITING IN SOCIAL STUDIES: SAMPLE UNIT PLAN AND ASSESSMENT OF STUDENT WRITING

The subject area objectives are the starting point for planning. Consider the concepts that students are to learn and then think about the best ways that writing can be used to foster students' learning of these concepts. In this example, students learn how values and beliefs affected the lifestyles of various groups of people in ancient Greece. They explore this topic more fully by reading books and looking at websites, and by taking on roles of citizens in drama activities about ancient Greece. They also go on a field trip to a local museum. They take notes from all these activities using the Note Taking: Completing Sentence Stems template (BLM 3.4). They further develop and demonstrate their knowledge by writing a story. Look at and assess students' writing to determine the writing skills you need to teach (writing dialogue, using commas, and so on). These skills, along with helping students to take notes and plan their stories, are the topics for mini-lessons.

Charts A1, A2, A3, A4, and A5 at the end of this appendix show the teacher's plan for the assignment, Jessica's note taking and character development planning, as well as her writing and how her teacher assessed her writing.

INTEGRATING POETRY WRITING IN HEALTH: SAMPLE UNIT PLAN AND ASSESSMENT OF STUDENT WRITING

In this sample unit plan, students learn about the harmful substances in tobacco, its addictive qualities, and the harmful effects on general health. Students explore this topic more fully by reading books, pamphlets, magazines, and web sites, and by listening to a health nurse. They take notes using BLM 3.6 template entitled Notes and Thoughts. They further develop and demonstrate their knowledge by writing a poem. Because students have not done previous poetry writing, the teacher teaches mini-lessons on basic poetry writing skills using repetition and creating titles for poems using the note-taking format.

Charts A6, A7, A8, and A9 at the end of this appendix show the teacher's plan for the assignment, Ashif's note taking, his writing, and the teacher's assessment of his writing.

INTEGRATING NON-NARRATIVE WRITING INTO SCIENCE: SAMPLE UNIT PLAN AND ASSESSMENT OF STUDENT WRITING

In this sample unit plan, students learn about levers, gears, and pulleys. They explore this topic more fully by reading books and looking at websites, by classifying everyday examples of each, and by doing hands-on activities to make simple machines out of a variety of objects. They take part in a competition making catapults that shoot wrapped chocolates into a tub. Students take notes using the Cornell Note-Taking Framework (BLM 3.8). They further develop and demonstrate their knowledge by writing in whatever genre they choose. Because students can choose any genre, the topics of mini-lessons are: assessing the validity of information, proofreading their writing for spelling, and using the Cornell note-taking framework.

Charts A10, A11, A12, and A13 at the end of this appendix show the teacher's plan for the assignment, Brandon's note taking, his writing, and the teachers assessment of his writing.

CHARTS FOR USE WITH APPENDIX A

....

GRADE 6 SOCIAL STUDIES: TEACHER'S PLAN

Topic: An Ancient Civilization

Subject Area Knowledge: Students will demonstrate an understanding of how values and beliefs in early civilizations affected people's daily lives.

Writing Objectives: Students will write dialogue that is easy to follow and develops character and advances the plot. They will use commas effectively.

Writing Activity: Students will write a story based in Classical Greece that shows how values and beliefs in early civilizations affected people's daily lives.

Activities for Gathering Information: Reading books, using the Internet, drama activity taking roles of citizens in Ancient Greece, field trip. Use the Note Taking: Completing Sentence Stems template to take notes on elements of daily life of various groups of people in Classical Greece.

Mini-Lessons:

1. Note Taking: Completing sentence stems (p. 18)

2. Allowing characters to lead the way (p. 45)

3. Developing characters and plot through dialogue (p. 45)

4. Inductive teaching of commas (p. 54)

....

A.1

JESSICA'S NOTES

Note Taking: Completing Sentence Stems

Topic: How class structure affected the way in which people living in Classical Greece were able to meet their needs

Sources Used: <www.historyforkids.org/greekciv/dailylife/htm>; Moulton, C. (Ed.). *Ancient Greece and Rome*. Princeton, NJ: Charles Scribner's Sons, 1998.

I learned that Greeks owned slaves that were prisoners of war. These slaves did the work in the fields, in the households, in government, in the mines, and in the marketplace. Some slaves had highly developed skills.

I will show readers how some unfree labourers worked to pay off debts.

My readers will need to know:

- that Greek women couldn't vote or own property. Rich women could only go out with a slave as a chaperone.

- that peasants were artisans and craftsmen. Many peasants paid rent to a wealthy landowner, though some owned land as a reward for military service or through inheritance.

A.2

JESSICA'S PLANNING SHEET FOR DEVELOPING CHARACTERS

Names:	Pericles	Pandora
Who is this character?	son of citizen	slave woman who works in a fish stall in the market
How does the character stand out?	gets lost when father takes him to the market	is trying to run away from her owner because he beats her
What is the character's personality?	kind hearted when he sees others in trouble	intelligent and courageous

A.3

JESSICA'S WRITING: CITIZEN'S SON HELPS SLAVE WOMAN

"Pericles, your father is waiting for you," his mother warned. Don't make him late for the Assembly."

Pericles ran to the door. Clutching his leather hoop and clay ball. He closed the door of their sun-dried brick house and stepped into the street. This was the first time he was going to his cousins new house. His father said Pericles could play with his cousin all day while his father was at the assembly where citizens debated and passed laws.

Pericles troted beside his father he noticed all the women with slaves as their chaperones. Soon they where in the market. Suddenly, he saw a man whiping the slave who sold fish in his stall. He stopped to watch what was happening. Not noticing that his father had kept walking.

"That's the last time you'll run away from me, Pandora. I don't know why I bring you to market. From now on, I'll keep you locked up in the house doing housework," the man cried as he whipped Pandora hard along her back.

Pericles looked around to tell his father that they should do something to help. But he only saw peasant farmers selling food from the land they had inherited or got as a reward for serving in the military.

"Great," thought Pericles, now how am I suppost to get to my cousins house?"

He saw Pandora looking defiently at her owner. She threw a fish on the table peasant woman to buy. Her owner turned around to serve the woman and Pandora ran as fast as she could into the crowd. Pericles watched her dart behind a cart piled high with olives.

"Where did she go?" her owner roared.

"She went in that direction, sir," Pericles pointed in the opposite direction. The man lumbered of. He left the unfree labourer. Who worked to pay off a debt he owed the man to sell the fish.

Suddenly, Pericles' father was standing over him. "So you've been standing here all along, Pericles. Why didn't you follow me? I was almost out of the market before I realized you weren't beside me."

"Sorry father," Pericles said. "I was watching some people. I should have stayed closer to you."

Pandora watched everything that happened. She nodded to Pericles as he and his father walked past the cart she was hiding behind. Then she walked off to a new life. She was no longer a slave because her owner never found her again.

A.4

JESSICA'S WRITING: ASSESSING CONTENT AREA NARRATIVE WRITING

Content	Points out of 4
1. Provides information about all the concepts	3
2. Provides accurate information about the concepts, so it is clear the writer understands the concepts	4
3. Creates a context that presents a thoughtful, and perhaps new, way of looking at the concept	4
4. Supporting details enhance character development, setting, and plot. The writing is easy to understand and creative/engaging	3
5. Consistently shows connections among the concepts	4
6. Uses multiple sources of information	2
7. Dialogue is natural, develops character, and moves the plot forward	4
8. Content information is woven into the writing in a way that does not disrupt the flow of the story	4
9. Story has a clear focus and is easy to follow	4

Organization	
1. Story events and ideas flow, are clearly connected, and are easy to follow	4
2. Lead provides sufficient information to bring readers into the story in an engaging way	4
3. Satisfying ending ties events together	3

Style	
1. Specific words and expressions engage readers	4
2. Use of language gives readers a sense of the writer	4
3. Uses a variety of simple, compound, and complex sentences	4

Conventions	
1. Consistently and effectively uses spelling, grammar and punctuation	3
Total	**59/64 = 92%**

A.5

Content

Jessica has included accurate information about members of the peasantry, the citizens of the wealthy class, unfree labourers, and women. She incorporated her notes directly into her writing. (This could be an area for a mini-lesson, as I would like Jessica to learn to use the information in her notes in her own words to a greater degree.) The information about the four groups of people is woven smoothly into the story and the focus of the story is maintained throughout. Jessica teaches readers about ancient Greece and tells a story at the same time.

She uses dialogue effectively to move the plot forward and explains what is happening (e.g., first sentence sets the scene, the slave-owner's dialogue shows what happened to Pandora, and Pericles' dialogue shows how he helped Pandora escape her owner).

Jessica provides some specific supporting details about why Pericles is accompanying his father through the market. I have a fairly good sense of why Pandora and her owner do what they do, but would like more information about Pericles to understand his motives for his actions.

Organization

The characters' actions and the events are generally connected. The problem is resolved, though it seems that the ending is rather abrupt. More information about Pericles' involvement in Pandora's life would fill in the gaps.

Style

Jessica uses specific words and expressions in a lively way (e.g., "warned," "trotted," "defiantly"). Although the sentences are not always punctuated correctly, she uses many complex sentences (e.g., "His father said Pericles could play with his cousin all day while his father was at the assembly where citizens debated and passed laws.") and an effective variety of simple and compound sentences.

Conventions

Jessica's writing meets grade level expectations because her spelling, grammar, and punctuation are generally correct. Errors arise when she does not double consonants of verbs when adding suffixes, for the word "were" and a word that she has not likely encountered often in her reading: "defiantly."

Her punctuation of dialogue is partially correct in most instances. Reinforcement of the generalizations learned in the mini-lesson is needed. Jessica's complex sentences are sometimes separated into fragments, though she punctuates simple and compound sentences correctly and uses correct grammar. (This could be an idea for a mini-lesson, as Jessica could benefit from instruction on ways to avoid using sentence fragments when writing complex sentences.)

A.5 (cont'd)

GRADE 4 HEALTH: TEACHER'S PLAN

Topic: Harmful Effects of Smoking

Subject Area Knowledge: Students will identify harmful substances in tobacco, show what *addiction* means, and describe the health effects of smoking.

Writing Objectives: Students will use repetition and write a title for their poetry.

Writing Activity: Students will write a poem showing the health effects of smoking.

Activities for Gathering Information: Students will read books, pamphlets, magazines, and use the Internet. They will hear a presentation by the health nurse and use the Notes and Thoughts template to take notes.

Mini-Lessons:

1. How to take notes using a Notes and Thoughts template (p. 18)

2. Using repetition in poetry writing (p. 32)

3. Writing titles for poetry (p. 33)

A.6

ASHIF'S NOTES

Topic: Harmful effects of smoking

Sources Used: <www.cancer.org/docroot/PED/ped_10_1.asp?sitearea=PED>; health nurse presentation

Notes	Thoughts
• Each year, nearly 1 of every 5 deaths in USA related to smoking.	
• About 87% of lung cancer deaths caused by smoking. Lung cancer is leading cause of cancer death and one of the most difficult to treat.	If everyone quit smoking, there would be a lot more people still alive.
• Smoking causes heart disease, lung, larynx, oral, esophagus, bladder, and pancreas cancer.	Why would anyone want to take something that is poisonous?
• Tobacco products contain nicotine. Nicotine is addictive and poisonous. More than 60 compounds that cause cancer are found in cigarettes—include ammonia, tar, and carbon monoxide.	So that's why people who smoke have a hard time running and climbing stairs and stuff.
• Carbon monoxide is emitted (400 times greater than what is considered safe in industrial settings). Carbon monoxide interferes with ability of blood to transport oxygen to body.	
• In 1988, the US Surgeon General said that being addicted to nicotine is like being addicted to drugs such as heroin and cocaine.	My uncle has been smoking for 35 years. He says he can't quit. He's addicted.

A.7

ASHIF'S POEM ON HARMFUL EFFECTS OF SMOKING: SMOKE AND YOU'LL BE SORRY!

Tobacco has nicotine, nicotine,
Don't know it's addictive —
Where have you been?

Smoking is harmful.
You'll get heart disease and cancer.
Yes sir,
The carbon monoxide messes up
Blood carrying oxygen.
Don't make me say it again.

Tobacco has nicotine, nicotine.
And it is addictive —
You know what I mean!

A.8

ASHIF'S POEM: ASSESSING CONTENT AREA POETRY WRITING

Content	Points out of 4
1. Provides information about all the concepts	3
2. Provides accurate information about all the concepts, so it is easy to see that the writer understands the concepts	3
3. Creates a context that presents a thoughtful, and perhaps new, way of looking at the concept	3
4. Provides specific supporting details consistently, so the writing is easy to understand and creative/engaging	2
5. Consistently shows connections among the concepts	3
6. Uses multiple sources of information	2
7. Says a lot with few words	3
8. If titles are used, they contribute to the overall meaning	4

Organization	
1. Ideas flow smoothly and are easy to follow	4
2. Line breaks add to the meaning and make the poem easy to follow	4

Style	
1. Creates images through one or more of the senses	3
2. Plays with rhythms and sounds of language	4
3. Uses language that gives a sense of the writer	4
4. Uses repetition to emphasize ideas or add to the rhythm of the poem	4

Conventions	
1. Consistently and effectively uses spelling, grammar, and punctuation	4
Total	**50/60 = 83%**

A.9

Content

Ashif's poem provides specific information about a few harmful effects of smoking (e.g., heart disease, cancer, blood can't carry oxygen as efficiently).

He identifies nicotine and carbon monoxide as harmful substances in cigarettes and cigarette smoke. He uses the word *addictive* but does not show what it means. His notes and thoughts show that he had more information to use in his poem and that he knows what *addictive* means, but Ashif didn't convey this knowledge in his poem. He had many resources available to him, but chose to take notes only from one website and the health nurse's presentation.

He uses specific vocabulary related to harmful effects of smoking and his poem is focused on one topic. Ashif has taken the extraneous words out—he does say something with a few words, but there's not a lot of substance to his message. His title clearly gives the message that smoking is harmful.

Organization

Ashif uses line breaks to emphasize important words and to help readers read the poem smoothly. The ideas flow smoothly, and it is easy to follow the message he conveys.

Style

The writing is lively and filled with Ashif's voice. He has done an excellent job of using repetition of sounds and words to enhance the rhythm and the flow of the poem. He uses some specific vocabulary to create visual images of the harmful effects of smoking.

Conventions

Ashif uses punctuation artfully to enhance the meaning of his poem. I showed him how to use the m-dash in a student-teacher conference, and he applied what he learned really well. His spelling is correct throughout the poem.

A.9 (cont)

GRADE 8 SCIENCE: TEACHER'S PLAN

Topic: Simple Machines

Subject Area Knowledge: Students will demonstrate an understanding of:

- mechanical advantage
- types of levers, pulleys, and gears
- how each simple machine makes work easier

Writing Objectives: Students will assess the validity of information they gather and proofread their writing for spelling.

Writing Activity: Students will write using a genre of their choice about two types of simple machines.

Activities for Gathering Information: Reading books and using the Internet, making catapults and other simple machines, classifying everyday simple machines. Students will use the Cornell note-taking framework to take notes.

Mini-Lessons:

1. Assessing the quality of information (p. 16)
2. Using Cornell note-taking framework (p. 18)
3. Deductive teaching of proofreading skills for spelling (p. 54)

A.10

BRANDON'S NOTES

Topic: How pulleys and levers work

Source Used: <http://www.sirinet.net/~jgjohnso/simple.html>

Questions	Notes
How do pulleys work?	• Pulley is a grooved wheel that turns around an axle (Fulcrum), a rope or a chain is used in the grove to lift heavy objects
	• Pulley changes the direction of the Force—Instead of lifting up, you can pull down using your body weigh against the load (what you are lifting) Examples—On Top of the Flag Pole to Raise and Lower the Flag, To Hoist a Sail, to Open Curtains
How do levers work?	• Lever is a bar that is free to turn about a fixed point called the Fulcrum. Has 2 other parts—force (what you are trying to move or lift)—effort arm—The work done on the lever.
	• First Class Lever has fulcrum between the effort and load (e.g., seesaw, scissors) Effort goes down in order to lift the Load.
	• Second Class has the load between the effort and the fulcrum. Produce a gain in force. Ex. wheelbarrow, bottle opener
	• Third Class has effort between load and fulcrum. Loss in force, but gain in speed and distance. Examples: broom, shovel, fishing pole, baseball bat

Short Summary of Notes

Pulleys are ropes around grooved wheels that change direction of force to lift things. Three types of levers have load, effort and fulcrum in different positions to lift or move things or to produce a gain in force or make things go faster and farther.

A.11

BRANDON'S NEWSPAPER ARTICLE: PULLEYS USED TO RESCUE STRANDED WHALES

There was a large commotion last week at the coast near the town of Fake Lake. A large group of whales had been stranded on the shores of the beach. This presented a problem of not enough space for patrons seeking an afternoon of fun in the sun. The bigger problem was that the rescue team had to return the whales to the water before they died.

They tried every idea that came to their mind, including pushing the whale with a tractor and offering the whale $50.00 to just get up and swim back into the water. All failed miserably. Time was running out when Pat Mercury, a concerned passer-by, proposed that they implement a pulley system to lift and carry the whales to safety. Pat explained that a construction crane would do the work because cranes are designed to lift large amounts of weight.

The rescue workers hooked the whales and raised them one-by-one. They positioned the whales above a safe amount of water, lowered them into the water and detached the hoist. The whales were saved! The rescue team was befuddled as to why they did not think of this earlier. If it were not for a knowledgeable stranger's assistance, the whales would surely have perished. With that in mind, the members of the rescue team resigned, sure that staying on duty would hurt more than help.

A.12

BRANDON'S NEWSPAPER ARTICLE: ASSESSING CONTENT-AREA WRITING

Content	Points out of 4
1. Provides information about all concepts	1
2. Provides accurate information about all concepts	2
3. Creates a context that presents a thoughtful, and perhaps new, way of looking at the concept	3
4. Provides specific supporting details consistently, so the writing is easy to understand and creative/engaging	1
5. Consistently shows connections among the concepts	2
6. Maintains a clear focus	3
7. Uses multiple sources of information	1

Organization

1. Beginning and ending clearly identify what writer is trying to achieve	2
2. Uses the structure of the genre to communicate effectively	3
3. Readers get a clear sense of the writer's voice	4

Style

1. Uses language appropriate for the audience and genre	3
2. Uses specific words and expressions, a variety of sentence structures/line breaks/graphic design in a creative and effective way	3

Conventions

1. Consistently and effectively uses spelling, grammar, and punctuation	4
Total	32/52 = 62%

A.13

Content

Brandon had much more information about levers and pulleys in his notes than he was able to incorporate into his newspaper article. (I will plan mini-lessons teaching students how to incorporate content information into newspaper articles and narratives in the next unit.) He created an interesting context for using a pulley and provided some accurate supporting details about how pulleys work, but did not include any information about levers. The article was focused on the rescue of the whales, and there were connections between ideas. There aren't many science ideas, so I cannot get a good sense of the connections he is making among science concepts. Brandon used only one source of information for his notes.

Organization

Brandon introduces the whale problem in the first paragraph, shows how the rescue workers tried to solve the problem in the second paragraph and then explains how they finally rescued the whales in the final paragraph. The title also summarizes the main idea of the newspaper article. In this respect, Brandon used the structure of the genre quite effectively. He just did not clearly achieve the purpose of demonstrating what two simple machines are and what they can be used for.

Style

Brandon uses specific language, such as *stranded, patrons*, and *construction crane* and readers get a clear sense of his voice through the humorous ending. There is a variety of sentence structures, as Brandon uses compound, complex and simple sentences. He uses short sentences for effect (e.g., "The whales were saved!"). He uses an appositive correctly.

The tone and language are generally appropriate for a newspaper article, though some details seem more like a narrative than a newspaper article (e.g., "This presented a problem of not enough space for patrons seeking an afternoon of fun in the sun.")

Conventions

Brandon uses punctuation, spelling and grammar effectively to make it easy for readers to follow his ideas. Even the less commonly used words are spelled correctly and the complex sentences are punctuated correctly.

A.13 (cont'd)

This workshop for parents, entitled Helping Your Children with their Writing, has been presented to parents who asked their teachers for some suggestions for working at home with their children on their writing. The PowerPoint slides, handouts and workshop notes are included in this appendix as a package for you to use to present a workshop to parents of your students. Please don't consider this to be a script for your presentation. These notes are intended to be background information that you can use along with the slides. The slides shown can be made into overhead transparencies, or you can download the slide presentation from the Portage & Main Press website <www.pandmpress.com> (go to the search box and insert the title of this book).

This workshop can run from 45 to 90 minutes, depending on how much time you choose to spend reading and commenting on the student writing with parents. The purpose of the workshop is to provide parents with information about what writers do and need to help them to become better writers. Parents will:

- learn about what to look for in their children's writing through reading two students' writing

- become familiar with types of questions and approaches they can take when talking with their children about their writing

- have their questions answered about how spelling, punctuation, and grammar are taught and learn how they can help their children improve their use of mechanics

- have their questions answered about their children's use of computers to write

Since the 1970s, researchers have watched successful writers and asked them to voice their thinking while they wrote. Their goal was to find out what writers do. Teachers have used what these researchers learned to teach children to write. What they found is that writers plan out what they want to say. They think about who their readers will be and what their readers will be expecting or hoping to get from the writing. Writers may write these ideas down in a list, an outline or a web, on scraps of paper, in a notebook or on their computer. Some writers talk to other people to figure out what they want to say and others let the ideas roll around in their head. Some planning happens before the writer starts to write, but often writers find they need to make changes to the plans as the writing goes along.

They think about what type of writing will be best to achieve what they want to do with their writing. Will a story, a poem, a letter, an essay, or another form work the best? Should there be words only or should there be photographs, drawings or other graphics?

Helping your Children with Their Writing

Slide 1

Plan for the Workshop

- What writers do and need
- What to look for in children's writing
- What to talk about with your children
- Spelling, grammar and punctuation
- Writing and computers

Slide 2

What Writers Do

- Plan what they want to say or accomplish with their writing
- Think about the best type of writing for their purpose and audience
- Write, read and think about what they have written, revise, and edit

Slide 3

What Writers Need

- Some choice of topic, audience, and genre to feel a sense of commitment
- Opportunities and resources to find information about the topic
- Quiet, unhurried time to think about what they want to say
- Time to write
- Opportunities to talk to others about their writing

Slide 4

How should the words and visuals be placed on the page? There is no one way that writers plan, but planning is something that all successful writers do.

They also write and look back over what they have written to see if they are saying what they want to say. They think about what they've written and if they're not satisfied with the way they've written their ideas or the way the writing is going, they go back and change what they've written. They may add, change, rearrange, or cut words and sentences. Some writers edit incorrect spelling, punctuation, and grammar as they go and others wait until they have finished.

Writing is hard work. To work through the idea blocks and the difficulties that writers have in finding the right word or in putting words together so they say what writers want to say, there has to be something in it for the writer. Having a choice in the topic, in the genre, and in the audience for the writing helps to create a sense of commitment to the writing. Writers need to believe that the project is worth writing. They need to feel that it's worthwhile to stick with the writing project until they produce a product they are proud of. This doesn't mean that writers have to have a choice of any topic or genre in the world all the time. Often, having a choice among two or three topics or among two or three genres and audiences is enough. It's important not to have so many restrictions on what student writers can write that there's little room for their own imaginations and interests to guide their writing.

Once topics and genres are chosen, writers need unhurried time to explore and learn more about them, and to write and talk about their writing. Writers also need a chance to run ideas past a peer or the teacher or to get feedback on whether a phrase or

What to Look For in Children's Writing	What to Look For in Children's Writing

• It's clear that the writer has something to say
 	
• There's a sense of the writer's own style/personality/way of thinking in the writing
	• The writer:
	  ○ says something using enough details
	  ○ organizes ideas so readers can follow them
	  ○ uses words and phrases, and a variety of sentence structures that keep readers interested
	  ○ uses spelling, punctuation and grammar that readers recognize.

Slide 5   Slide 6

paragraph says what writers want them to say. There should be quiet time for writing and thinking, and there should be a space to talk with others.

Slides 5 and 6 can be used with either one or two samples of student writing. I have included a narrative written by a grade-8 student, "Mechanical Advantage Haunts You" (from BLM 6.1) and a grade-5 informational piece, "Soil Erosion and How to Avoid It" (from BLM 4.10). Invite parents to read and then discuss with you their impressions of how well the writer of "Mechanical Advantage Haunts You" achieves the characteristics of good writing identified in slides 5 and 6.

In my view, the author, Craig, a grade-8 student, wanted to inform readers about the three classes of levers, and about pulleys and gears in a humorous and entertaining way. He also sent a message that those who remain ignorant of the workings of mechanical advantage do so at their peril.

We get a sense of Craig's sense of humour and his wit when you read such phrases such as "Soon he began to forget what mechanical advantage really was and was simply lost in a world of hard work" and "Jim was quickly sucked into what seemed to be . . . a science classroom." He uses punctuation as well as words to add to the sense that the events were extraordinary and hard to believe. We also get a sense that Craig has a fondness for literature and literary language, as he has created a spoof on Dickens's *A Christmas Carol*, and uses phrases such as "Alas, the uneducated mortal has arrived." Jim's final realization, that he "really need[s] to lay off the junk food" is a humorous touch that could easily be attributed to modern teenagers. The writer clearly says something using enough details.

Craig establishes Jim's lazy and uncurious character by telling us so and by showing that he had a hard life because he wasn't very strong and didn't use mechanical advantage. The dialogue between the ghosts and Jim provide details about the simple machines, although anyone having a superficial knowledge of each might still need more information to fully understand them. The writer clearly organizes ideas so readers can follow them.

Craig has used the progression of the three ghosts' visits to organize ideas. The framework is familiar to readers who know Dickens's story, but, on top of this, three is a number that has been used by storytellers across the ages and across continents. Craig followed in a time-honoured tradition by having three ghosts talk about three different aspects of mechanical advantage. The beginning of the story shows Jim's shortcomings, and events build to an ending where the ghosts help Jim to overcome those shortcomings. The writer clearly uses words and phrases, and a variety of sentence structures, that keep readers interested.

Craig used colourful phrases, such as those identified, to describe his style. He used extraordinary words, such as "swirling vortex," but didn't overuse them so that his writing seemed contrived. Craig used a lot of literary language to create a sense that the

Craig's Story (Grade 8)

Mechanical Advantage Haunts You

Jim was a very lazy and ignorant kid. "Who needs mechanical advantage!" he would always say. Of course, this always made his life harder, especially since he wasn't that strong himself. Soon he began to forget what mechanical advantage really was, and was simply lost in a world of hard work. He couldn't keep up with it, and his laziness only made matters worse.

It seemed that there was no hope left for this poor soul. Fortunately for him, though, he was being watched. And hope would come sooner than he thought. One night he fell asleep, but right after he fell asleep, he found himself sitting on his bed.

"Ah, this is one odd dream," he said to himself. He turned around to see him or what seemed to be his "body" sleeping on his bed.

Slide 7

"OK, this is getting weird," he said. It would soon get weirder, for a shadowy figure emerged out of nowhere. Jim couldn't help letting out a high, girlish cry for help.

"SILENCE!" said the figure. "I, the Ghost of Pulleys have appeared before you today to teach you a lesson. I am one of the three Ghosts of Mechanical Advantage. You have been very foolish lately, being ignorant about the power of mechanical advantage! Prepare to be educated!"

Jim was quickly sucked into what seemed to be... a science classroom? There, standing in front of him was the Ghost of Pulleys.

"Now, it is time for your enlightenment. The pulley can greatly help you by reducing the force needed to lift an object," Jim slowly but surely began to understand how helpful pulleys were: moveable pulleys, fixed pulleys, double pulleys, the works.

"So, the more sections of rope I have, the easier it is to lift?" Jim asked.

"Of course," replied the ghost.

Slide 8

After an adequate lesson with the Ghost of Pulleys, Jim was sent to the next ghost. A swirling vortex opened up before him and he jumped in. Whoosh! Jim landed in a playground where he saw a see-saw in the middle, and a bunch of other things lying around, such as a hockey stick, a pair of shears, a hammer, and a crowbar.

"Alas, the uneducated mortal has arrived," sounded a booming voice.

"Let me guess," Jim replied, "The Ghost of Levers."

The ghost was very pleased, "Ah, that gets a lot of things out of the way. Now, it is time for your enlightenment." Jim was told about Class 1, Class 2 and Class 3 levers, as well as how you can find them in real life.

"Yes, levers can help you greatly when used correctly. Now for your final destination." The vortex appeared before Jim again and he jumped in, wondering what was next. Tick-Tock, Tick-Tock, Tick-Tock.

"Where am I??" Jim said in exasperation. His surroundings were quite different from the last two. First the classroom, then the playground, but now... inside a clock tower? There were gears everywhere, all kinds of gears, all working together to make the clock precisely accurate. Suddenly, a shadowy figure leaped out from behind one of the gears.

Slide 9

"Howdy there, partner! You ready for some gear education?"

"Sure, I'm guessing the gear ghost, right?" replied Jim.

"Right you are," said the ghost. The ghost quickly launched him to the top of the tower and proceeded to explain all about gears: driver gears, follower gears, even rack and pinion gears. At the end of his lesson with the gear ghost, a vortex appeared and sucked him in without warning.

After a couple of seconds, he was quickly sent to his room, and returned to the position he was in before on the bed. In front of him were the three ghosts. The Ghost of Pulleys stepped forward, took a deep breath and said, "Use the knowledge you have just learned to assist you in daily life."

Then the Ghost of Levers stepped forward and said, "Do not forget what we have taught you."

And finally the Ghost of Gears stepped forward and said, "I reckon we could do this again sometime. We'll be here if you're ever in need." The three ghosts quickly huddled together and before you could say "mechanical advantage," they disappeared.

Jim sighed and then climbed into his bed. "Wow," he said, "I really need to lay off the junk food."

Slide 10

ghosts took their mission to enlighten Jim about mechanical advantage very seriously. For example, he wrote, "Use the knowledge you have just learned to assist you in daily life." Craig uses a variety of sentence structures, including simple sentences (e.g., "Jim was a very lazy and ignorant kid"), many compound sentences (e.g., "Then the Ghost of Levers stepped forward and said, 'Do not forget what we have taught you'"), and some complex sentences (e.g., "After an adequate lesson with the Ghost of Pulleys, Jim was sent to the next ghost"). Craig uses spelling, punctuation and grammar that readers recognize. He uses conventional spelling throughout for commonly used words and out-of-the-ordinary words such as *vortex*.

If there is sufficient time, invite parents to read the piece written by Cristina, a grade-5 student, and then discuss in small groups their impressions of the piece using the same criteria. Follow this up with a whole-group discussion.

In my view, Cristina makes the point quite emphatically that soil erosion has detrimental effects. There's a sense of the writer's own style/personality/way of thinking in the writing. I get the sense that Cristina likes to express herself in a straightforward, forceful manner. She lets her audience know that she's serious about her topic, insisting that we not "take soil for granted" and that "we don't have to let that happen." She seems to be unflinching as she talks directly to her readers and instructs us on what we should do to prevent soil erosion. It's clear that the writer says something using enough details.

In my view, Cristina has made a very clear point, bringing it home by giving details about how soil "will not always be under your feet if you allow wind and rain to let it erode," together with information about how the wind and rain cause erosion. She

Cristina's Report (Grade 5)

Soil Erosion and How to Avoid It

Dont take soil for granted. It will not always be under your feet if you allow wind and rain to let it erode. Whenever it rains. The raindrops move soil. Whenever it is windy. The wind picks up the soil and moves it.

People make soil erode faster by doing certain things. When farmers allow cows sheep and horses to eat the grass down to the dirt, or when they plow the soil to much so its like powder. They make soil erosion happen faster. People who cut down all the trees on a hill make the soil looser so it will erode faster. Once soil is gone, plants have nothing to grow in.

Cristina's Report (continued)

We don't have to let that happen. Soil erosion can be prevented by planting trees to make wind breaks and by leaving grass strips between plots of land that have been ploughed. Plants and trees prevent soil erosion. They slow down rain water so that it soaks into the ground rather than pushing the soil along. The roots also hold the soil down so it cant be washed away.

Think about soil erosion whenever you dig up plants or trees or whenever you dig in the dirt. If you let the wind and rain Wash all the soil away, what will be left of your backyard?

(Unedited version)

Slide 11

explains how people do certain things to hasten erosion and gives specifics on how to prevent erosion. The writer clearly organizes ideas so readers can follow them.

I find the paragraphs are set up to make it easy to see what the issue is (introduced in the first paragraph), how people contribute (in the second paragraph), what people can do to avoid causing soil erosion (in the third paragraph) and then giving readers something to think about so they can take action in future (fourth paragraph). The writers clearly use words and phrases, and sentence structures, that keep readers interested.

The language is appropriate for the topic (words like *windbreaks, ploughed, soaks, washed away*). Although not particularly colourful, the words and phrases explain the concepts clearly and accurately. Cristina uses a variety of simple sentences (e.g., "Plants and trees prevent soil erosion"), and complex sentences (e.g., "Whenever it is windy, the wind picks up the soil and moves it"). The writer clearly uses spelling, punctuation, and grammar that readers recognize. Cristina has used conventional spelling, punctuation, and grammar throughout her paper.

The first question in slide 12 focuses your talk about your children's writing on the content, on what they're trying to say. When experienced writers talk to others about their writing, they want to know if their message is getting across and if their readers are finding their writing worth reading. When your children see that the most important thing about their writing is that they say something important to themselves and say it in ways that engage their readers, they'll be more motivated to revise and edit their writing.

The second and third questions in slide 12 could focus on any aspect of the writing—the ideas, dialogue, organization, format on the page, use of language, opening sentence, etc.

When you talk with your children about their writing, you can also give your impressions. Writers benefit from knowing how their writing is being understood and enjoyed by readers. Slide 13 has some starting points for such discussions. These starting points give your children feedback on how well they are accomplishing what they set out to do with their writing. They're getting a chance to see what kind of impression readers get of their writing.

If parents were talking to Cristina, the grade-5 writer of the soil erosion piece, for example, they might provide feedback such as:

Talking With Your Children About their Writing: Global Questions	Talking With Your Children About their Writing: Starting Points
• What do you want to say in your writing? • What part of your writing are you most proud of? • What part of your writing do you think needs improvement?	• Here's what you're saying to me in your writing: • Here's what I think are the best parts of your writing: • Here's what I think are the parts that could be improved:

Slide 12   Slide 13

Here's what you're saying to me in your writing: You make your point very clearly—you want readers to think about what will happen to the soil if we dig up soil or uproot trees.

Here's what I think are the best parts of your writing: I like the repeated "whenever it" in the first paragraph. It almost sounds poetic and you give two specific examples of erosion. I also like how you mixed short and long sentences in the third paragraph. You wrote: "Plants and trees prevent soil erosion." Then you wrote, "They slow down rain water so that it soaks into the ground rather than pushing the soil along." It's easier for me to follow what you're saying when you have short and long sentences. If there were too many short sentences, it would be choppy. If there were too many long sentences, it would be hard to follow what you're saying.

Here's the part I think could be improved: In the second paragraph where you write that the soil gets looser when trees are cut down on the hill, I'm not sure what you mean by getting looser. What happens when trees are cut down on a hill? Let's look it up and see if you can find another way to explain what happens.

The second and third questions in slide 13 could highlight the clarity of the information and the understandings shown by the writer, as well as the writer's style, use of details, organization, and use of language. It's a good idea to start with these types of feedback, so children put a lot of thought and energy into the content and organization of their writing.

Mechanics are not to be overlooked, however. Slide 14 provides suggestions for helping young writers in this area. Often, writers can find errors on their own if they read their writing aloud to someone. When parents ask their children to read their writing to them, they should encourage their children to correct any errors they find as they read.

If errors remain, parents can best help their children to learn how to correct the errors and not make the errors again by not correcting every spelling, grammar, and punctuation error. When parents correct all the errors, their children often just copy the corrections into their good copy without putting a lot of thought into what the errors were and how to avoid them in future. Instead of making the corrections, it is a good idea to look for types of errors that the children make. Using Cristina's essay on soil erosion as an example, parents might identify and explain that she is not using apostrophes in contractions such as *don't* and *can't*. Then, parents could ask Cristina to look for other instances where she has written contractions and help her figure out where the apostrophe is needed.

Spelling, Punctuation and Grammar: Helping Your Children

- Ask your child to read the piece of writing aloud.

- Instead of correcting every error for your child, look for types of errors that your child makes.

- Ask your child to find and correct other errors of that type.

- Using spelling checkers effectively

Slide 14

Most Commonly Confused Homonyms

to	too	two
there	their	they're
its	it's	
through	threw	
no	know	
hours	ours	
wood	would	
herd	heard	

In addition, *where* and *were* are often confused, as are *of* and *off*.

Slide 15

Computers and Writing

- Influence of Instant Messaging on children's spelling, punctuation and grammar

- Acknowledging sources

- Determining the accuracy of website information

Slide 16

Evaluating Websites

Parents and their children might look for:
- the name of the website's author and publisher and the author's credentials
- contact information for the website's author
- the purpose and sponsors of the website
- who is advertising on the website, if there are advertisements
- evidence that the author has consulted a number of sources to find the information posted on the website
- links that are working and that lead to other authoritative websites
- current dates when the information was updated

Slide 17

This pattern could be repeated for the sentence fragments Cristina created when she wrote "Whenever it rains." Parents could point out that this phrase explains what has to happen in order for the rain to move the soil, so the phrase belongs with: "The raindrops move soil." Cristina could then look for another instance where she has created a sentence fragment from a clause and combine the two parts of the sentence.

She used the incorrect homonym—*to* instead of *too*. Parents could simply point this out and ask Cristina to make the correction. Cristina and her parents could figure out a way to remember when to use *too* in sentences.

There are some who believe that if children are writing on computers and using spell-checkers to correct their spelling, they will not learn to spell. There is no research showing this to be true. Instead, there is evidence that young writers correct almost 20 percent more of their spelling errors when they use computers that have spell-checkers.

There are limitations to the assistance that spell-checkers can provide, however. They can't distinguish between homonyms, so if a child types the incorrect homonym, the spell-checkers won't identify the error. Also, if the spelling errors are real words, the spell-checkers won't highlight the error. If the child's misspelling is not even close to the correct spelling, the choices offered by the spell-checkers will not include the correct one.

Parents can help their children use spell-checkers effectively by encouraging them to spell words phonetically if their spellings are so different from conventional spellings that the spell-checkers does not provide appropriate options. They can also help their children identify incorrectly used homonyms in their writing and then create lists of the words with drawings or actions that help the children remember when to use each homonym.

The Media Awareness Network survey of Canadian children in grades 4 to 11 in 2003 found that young people's use of instant messaging increases as students get older. Thirty-six percent of children in grades 4 and 5 said they chatted with friends on Instant Messaging, girls being twice as likely as boys to do so. By grades 8 and 9, 77 percent of girls and boys chat on IM. The percentage increases to 84 percent of young people in grades 10 and 11.

Because the keyboard is small and the messages are short and rattled off with no time taken for proofreading, there are many grammar and spelling mistakes and practically no punctuation in the messages sent through Instant Messaging. Lower-case letters are used exclusively, and many acronyms, such as lol (laugh out loud), are used. Teachers are seeing these writing practices creeping into classroom writing. Parents can help their children differentiate between the expectations for writing in classrooms and other formal settings and for writing in the informal Internet formats.

With the Internet and digital technology, it's becoming easier and easier to take someone else's words, drawings, photographs, sounds, music, and videos and use them in our own productions or compositions. The concept of *plagiarism*, which is the act of taking someone else's creative work and passing it off as your own without crediting the original source, is often not in the forefront of children's thoughts when they use the Internet to find information, images, music, etc. for their classroom assignments.

Parents can talk with their children about honouring the creators of the quotes and images they use by giving them credit for their creations. In the adult world, charges of plagiarism lead to public embarrassment and damage one's professional reputation. Parents can encourage their children to identify where the Internet quotes and images that they use in their compositions come from and make sure that they acknowledge the website URL and the name of the person who created them at the end of their compositions.

Today's children use the Internet at least as frequently as they use books to get information for their writing projects. Often, they are unaware that certain websites contain more accurate information than others and that some websites have a particular bias in their presentation of information. Parents can help their children ensure greater accuracy in the information they are gathering by encouraging them to go to three or four websites on a particular topic. The information from each website can be compared and contrasted. If there is conflicting information, children can identify which perspective or fact appears most often in the websites, but they can also evaluate the authority and objectivity of the website creators.

REFERENCES

McNaughton, D., C. Hughes, and N. Ofiesh. "Proofreading for Students with Learning Disabilities: Integrating Computer Use and Strategy Use. *Learning Disabilities Research and Practice* 12 (1997), 16–28.

Media Awareness Network. *Young Canadians in a Wired World: Phase II— Trends and Recommendations.* Ottawa: Retrieved on 1 June 2007 at <http://www.media-awareness.ca/english/research/YCWW/phaseII/ trends_recommendations.cfm>, 2005.

SCIENCE

Bardoe, C. *Gregor Mendel, the Friar Who Grew Peas.* New York: Abrams Books for Young Readers, 2006. [biography]

Busby, P. *First to Fly: How Wilbur and Orville Wright Invented the Airplane.* Markham, ON: Scholastic/Madison, 2002. [biography]

Cole, J. *The Magic School Bus Plays Ball: A Book About Forces.* Markham, ON: Scholastic, 1998. [narrative, explanation]

_____. *The Magic School Bus Explores the Senses.* Markham, ON: Scholastic Canada, 2001. [narrative, explanation]

Conlon, K. *Under the Ice: A Marine Biologist at Work.* Toronto: Kids Can Press, 2002. [autobiography, explanation]

Fisher, L.E. *Alexander Graham Bell.* New York: Atheneum, 1999. [biography, explanation]

Freedman, R. *The Wright Brothers: How they Invented the Airplane.* New York: Holiday House, 1991. [biography, explanation]

Gibbons, G. *Galaxies, Galaxies!* New York: Holiday House, 2007. [explanation]

Godkin, C. *Fire! The Renewal of a Forest.* Toronto: Fitzhenry and Whiteside, 2006. [narrative]

Hudson, C.W. *Construction Zone.* Cambridge, MA: Candlewick Press, 2006. [explanation, virtual tour]

Jenkins, S. *Prehistoric Actual Size.* Boston, MA: Houghton Mifflin, 2005. [explanation]

McClafferty, C.K. *Something Out of Nothing: Marie Curie and Radium.* New York: Farrar Straus Giroux, 2006. [biography]

Montgomery, S. *Quest for the Tree Kangaroo: An Expedition to the Cloud Forest of New Guinea.* Boston: Houghton Mifflin, 2006. [narrative, almost diary-like]

Sidman, J. *Song of the Water Boatman and Other Pond Poems.* Boston: Houghton Mifflin, 2005. [poetry, explanation]

Simon, S. *The Brain.* Toronto: HarperCollins, 1999. [explanation]

_____. *Out of Sight: Pictures of Hidden Worlds.* New York: Sea Star Books, 2000. [explanation]

_____. *Weather.* Toronto: HarperCollins, 2000. [explanation]

Slavin, B. *Transformed: How Everyday Things are Made*. Toronto: Kids Can Press, 2005. [procedures]

Thimmesh, C. *Team Moon: How 400,000 People Landed Apollo II on the Moon*. Boston, MA: Houghton Mifflin, 2006. [case studies]

Thornhill, J. *I Found a Dead Bird: The Kids' Guide to the Cycle of Life and Death*. Toronto: Maple Tree Press, 2006. [explanation]

Verstraete, L. *Accidental Discoveries: From Laughing Gas to Dynamite*. Markham, ON: Scholastic, 1999. [case studies]

Wick, W. *A Drop of Water*. New York: Scholastic, 1997. [explanation]

Zoehfeld, D.W. *What Is the World Made of? All about Solids, Liquids, and Gases*. Toronto: HarperCollins, 1998. [explanation]

SOCIAL STUDIES

Bailey, L. *Adventures in Ancient China*. Toronto: Kids Can Press, 2003. [narrative, explanation]

Charles, V.M. *The Birdman*. Toronto: Tundra, 2006. [biography]

Coleman, P. *Rosie the Riveter: Women Working on the Home Front in World War II*. New York: Random House, 1998. [explanation, case studies]

Granfield, L. *Pier 21: Gateway of Hope*. Toronto: Tundra, 2000. [explanation, case studies, commentary]

_____. *Where Poppies Grow: A World War I Companion*. Markham, ON: Fitzhenry and Whiteside, 2001. [poetry, explanation, letters]

Greenwood, B. *A Pioneer Story: The Daily Life of a Canadian Family in 1840*. Toronto: Kids Can Press, 1994. [narrative, explanation]

_____. *The Last Safe House: A Story of the Underground Railroad*. Toronto: Kids Can Press, 1998. [narrative, explanation, instructions]

_____. *Factory Girl*. Toronto: Kids Can Press, 2006. [narrative, case studies, commentary]

Hodge, D. *The Kids Book of Canada's Railway and How the CPR was Built*. Toronto: Kids Can Press, 2000. [explanation]

Hughes, S. *Coming to Canada: Building a Life in a New Land*. Toronto: Maple Tree Press, 2005. [case studies, explanation, timeline]

Levine, K. *Hana's Suitcase*. Toronto: Second Story Press, 2003. [narrative]

Marrin, A. *Saving the Buffalo*. New York: Scholastic Nonfiction, 2006. [explanation, commentary]

Moore, C. *The BIG Book of Canada: Exploring the Provinces and Territories*. Toronto: Tundra, 2002. [explanation]

Ross, V. *The Road to There: Mapmakers and their Stories*. Toronto: Tundra Books, 2003. [explanation, biography]

Scow, A., and A. Spalding. *Secret of the Dance*. Vancouver: Orca Book Publishers, 2006. [narrative, explanation]

Springer, J. *Listen to Us: The World's Working Children*. Toronto: Groundwood, 1997. [commentary, case studies]

Tanaka, S. *The Buried City of Pompeii: What it Was Like when Vesuvius Exploded*. Markham, ON: Scholastic, 1997. [narrative]

Yue, C., and D. Yue. *The Wigwam and the Longhouse*. Boston, MA: Houghton Mifflin, 2000. [case studies]

Zhang, A. *Red Land Yellow River: A Story from the Cultural Revolution.* Toronto: Groundwood, 2004. [autobiography]

MUSIC

Ardley, N. *A Young Person's Guide to Music.* London, UK: Dorling Kindersley, 2004. [audio book, explanation]

Freedman, R. *The Voice that Challenged a Nation: Marian Anderson and the Struggle for Equal Rights.* Boston, MA: Houghton Mifflin, 2004. [autobiography, commentary]

Hayes, A. *Meet the Orchestra.* New York: Harcourt, 2001. [explanation, with animal characters as musicians]

Kamen, G. *Hidden Music: The Life of Fanny Mendelssohn.* New York: Simon and Schuster, 1996. [biography]

Koscielniak, B. *The Story of the Incredible Orchestra.* Boston: Houghton Mifflin Company, 2000. [explanation]

Raschka, C. *Mysterious Thelonious.* Markham, ON: Scholastic Canada, 1997. [biography]

Reich, S. *Clara Schumann: Piano Virtuoso.* New York: Clarion Books, 1999. [biography]

ART

Bogart, J. *Emily Carr at the Edge of the World.* Toronto: Tundra, 2003. [biography]

Burleigh, R. *Seurat and La Grande Jatte.* New York: Harry N. Abrams Inc., 2004. [biography, explanation]

Scieszka, J. *Seen Art?* New York: Viking, 2005. [narrative]

Venezia, M. *Francisco Goya.* Markham, ON: Scholastic Canada, 2000. [biography]

Winter, J. *Diego.* New York: Knopf, 2007. [biography in English and Spanish]

HEALTH

Brown, L.K. *What's the Big Secret: Talking about Sex with Girls and Boys.* New York: Little Brown and Company, 2000. [explanation]

Cole, J. *The Magic School Bus Explores the Senses.* New York: Scholastic, 2001. [narrative, explanation]

Douglas, A., and J. Douglas. *Body Talk: The Straight Facts on Fitness, Nutrition and Feeling Great about Yourself!* Toronto: Maple Tree Press, 2002. [explanation]

Farrell, J. *Invisible Enemies: Stories of Infectious Disease.* New York: Farrar, Straus and Giroux, 2005. [explanation, biography, posters]

Graydon, S. *Made You Look: How Advertising Works and Why You Should Know.* Toronto: Annick Press, 2003. [explanation, instruction]

_____. *In Your Face: The Culture of Beauty and You.* Toronto: Annick Press, 2004. [explanation, commentary]

Romanek, T. *Squirt: The Most Interesting Book You'll Ever Read about Blood.* Toronto: Kids Can Press, 2006. [explanation]

Simon, S. *Guts: Our Digestive System.* New York: HarperCollins, 2005. [explanation]

_____. *The Brain: Our Nervous System.* New York: Morrow Junior Books, 2006. [explanation]

_____. *Lungs: Your Respiratory System.* New York: HarperCollins, 2007. [explanation]

MATHEMATICS

Anno, M., and M. Anno. *Anno's Mysterious Multiplying Jar*. New York: Puffin, 1999. [instruction]

Geisert, A. *Roman Numerals I to MM*. Boston, MA: Houghton Mifflin, 2001. [instruction]

Lasky, K. *The Librarian Who Measured the Earth*. Boston, MA: Little and Brown Company, 1994. [biography]

Metropolitan Museum of Art. *Museum Shapes*. New York: Little, Brown and Company, 2006. [explanation]

Nobisso, J. *The Numbers Dance: A Counting Comedy*. Westhampton Beach, NY: Gingerbread House, 2005. [poetry]

Schmandt-Besserat, D. *The History of Counting*. New York: Morrow Junior Books, 1999. [narrative, explanation]

Schwartz, D.M. *On Beyond a Million*. New York: Random House, 1999. [instruction, explanation]

Tang, G. *Math Appeal: Mind-Stretching Math Riddles*. New York: Scholastic, 2003. [instruction, riddles]

Wyatt, V. *The Math Book for Girls and Other Beings Who Count*. Toronto: Kids Can Press, 2000. [instruction, case studies, commentary]

Blackline Masters

INTEGRATING WRITING IN A CONTENT AREA UNIT

Integrating writing for a unit on: _____

Subject Area Concepts:

Writing Objectives:

Writing Activity:

Strategies for Gathering Information:

Mini-Lessons:

Resources for Gathering Information:

HOW ACCURATE IS INTERNET INFORMATION?

Use the following questions to help you decide what information you can trust and what information you should ignore.

1. What viewpoint does the information source seem to promote?

2. What different viewpoints are presented? Does the website creator fairly present each one?

3. What information seems to be missing? Whose viewpoints seem to be missing?

4. Are there any stereotypes? What are they? Why do you think the creator used stereotypes?

5. What information seems to be exaggerated (e.g., "Never before has anyone tried…") or overgeneralized (e.g., "Everyone knows that…")?

6. What credentials does the creator have to make her/him an expert on the topic?

7. What sources did the creator consult to make him/her more knowledgeable?

8. Is the information up to date?

9. Does the creator present opinions as facts? (e.g., "It is well known that…")

10. When you compare the information from three or four different sources, what contradictions do you find? How will you decide which information to use if there are contradictions?

ASKING GOOD INTERVIEW QUESTIONS

Directions: Ask yourself these two questions after you read each of the sample interview questions at the bottom of this chart.

1. Is the question open-ended enough so that the interviewee can give lots of information, or is it a closed-ended (yes/no) question?

2. Does the question clearly relate to the overall topic of the interview? If you answer no to either of these questions, revise the question so it is open-ended and related to the topic. Then, talk with a partner about what you have learned about how to create good interview questions.

Sample Topic: What do people think they should do, and what do they actually do, to stay healthy?

Sample Interview Questions

1. What physical activities do you do every day to stay healthy? What do you do just once or twice a week?

2. Do you like junk food?

3. Would you ever start smoking? Why or why not?

4. How much television do you watch on weekdays?

5. Do you think people should eat vegetables and fruit every day?

6. Are you worried about your weight?

7. What are you trying to do to live a healthier life?

DECIDING WHAT IS RELEVANT

Information from the book *Icebergs and Glaciers*, by Seymour Simon (unpaginated) New York: William Morrow, and Company, 1987	My thoughts about what is relevant to my question.
Question: What causes glaciers to move?	I'm looking for information about the causes of movement of glaciers.
In the early part of the twentieth century, Swiss and Italian scientists drilled holes straight down through the thickness of a glacier. Then they placed iron rods in the holes. Over the years, the scientists found that the rods bent at the top. This showed that the ice at the top of a glacier moves more quickly than the ice at the bottom.	This is interesting, but it explains only which part of the glacier moves more quickly, not what causes glaciers to move.
The thicker the glacier, the faster it moves. That's because the greater weight of the glacier causes the crystals of ice to creep more rapidly. Also, a steep glacier will flow much more quickly than one on level land.	The parts I've highlighted explain that the thickness of the glacier, the slope of the land the glacier is on, and the temperature of the glacier cause its movement.
Temperature is a third factor that affects the speed of a glacier. The warmer the glacier, the faster the ice moves, because there is a greater amount of meltwater beneath the ice. In fact, scientists sometimes group glaciers together depending upon whether they are cold or warm. But even "warm" glaciers are still freezing.	The highlighted parts opposite explain how temperature regulates the speed of a glacier. The unhighlighted parts provide additional information about warm and cold glaciers, but it doesn't explain what causes glaciers to move.

NOTE TAKING: COMPLETING SENTENCE STEMS

Topic: _____

Sources Used: _____

I learned that

I will show readers how

My readers will need to know that

I need to look for more information about

NOTE TAKING: COMPLETING SENTENCE STEMS—AN EXAMPLE

Topic: What the Underground Railroad was and how it helped slaves in the southern United States

I learned that:

- Harriet Tubman was a slave who escaped from a plantation to St. Catharines, in 1850

- songs like "Swing Low, Sweet Chariot," "Brother Moses Gone to de Promised Land," and "Follow the Drinkin' Gourd" gave directions on how to escape slavery to get to the northern states or to Canada

- the Quakers were part of the Underground Railroad. They raised money to buy clothes, feed the escaping slaves, and pay for boat and train rides

I will show readers how:

- the runaway slaves were helped by some white people and by freed slaves in the Underground Railroad. They called the places where runaway slaves would rest and eat "stations" and "depots." The people who helped were called "stationmasters" and "conductors."

My readers will need to know that:

- Congress passed the Fugitive Slave Law to help Southern slave owners bring back escaping slaves

I need to look for more information about:

- other conductors on the Underground Railroad: John Fairfield in Ohio, the son of a slaveholding family, and Levi Coffin, a Quaker, who assisted more than 3000 slaves

- how many people Harriet Tubman freed; one source says 300, and another says 750

- when the Underground Railroad started; one source says 1831 when Nat Turner revolted against slavery, and the other says 1810

Sources

Sadlier, R. *The Kids Book of Black Canadian History*. Toronto: Kids Can Press, 2003.

Public Broadcasting System website: <www.pbs.org/wgbh/aia/part4/4p2944.html>

NOTES AND THOUGHTS

Topic: _____

Sources: _____

_____

Notes	Thoughts

NOTES AND THOUGHTS—AN EXAMPLE

Topic: How do percussion instruments make sounds?

Sources: <www.cafemuse.com/soundgarden/makingmusic/percussion.htm>

<www.scott.k12.va.us/bmoorehouse/percussion.htm>

Notes	Thoughts
Part or all of the percussion instruments vibrate when they are struck, shaken, or scraped.	I know that sound is made of vibrations. I wonder if almost anything could be a percussion instrument if all you have to do is hit, shake, or scrape it. I'd like to try making different kinds of percussion instruments.
Two types: 1. melodic (plays melodies — like a vibraphone) 2. non-melodic (makes sounds that don't change in pitch)	I usually think of drums and shakers as being percussion instruments, but I didn't know that instruments like xylophones that play melodies were percussion instruments. All you do is hit them to make them vibrate, so I guess that makes them a percussion instrument.
Two parts: 1. primary vibrator — the part that creates sound (e.g., snare drum — membrane stretched across the metal frame) 2. resonant vibrator makes the sound louder (e.g., snare drum — the metal case)	It makes sense that the part you hit or scrape or that gets something shaken against it would be the primary vibrator — that's what makes the sound. I looked up the word *resonance*. It means that something continues to sound and the sound is deep and full. That must mean that, if you didn't have the resonant vibrator, the instrument would not be very loud and the sound would end quickly.

THE CORNELL NOTE-TAKING FRAMEWORK

Topic: _____

Sources: _____

_____

Questions	Notes

Short Summary of Notes (Analysis):

THE CORNELL NOTE-TAKING FRAMEWORK—AN EXAMPLE

Topic: World War I

Sources Used: Granfield, Linda. *Where Poppies Grow: A World War I Companion*. Markham, ON: Fitzhenry and Whiteside, 2001.

Questions	Notes
How and when did WWI start? (unanswered question: What countries besides Belgium, France, and Canada fought with Britain?) Where was the war fought? (unanswered question: What year did the US join the Allies?)	• started in August 1914, after heir to Austro-Hungarian throne was murdered in June 1914 • Germany invaded Belgium. Britain had to defend Belgians because of a treaty • in Belgium (e.g., Mons, Ypres) and France (e.g., Vimy, the Somme) • in trenches — three lines: the front line closest to the enemy, the support line, and the reserve line • at sea — German U-boats (submarines) sank supply ships from North America (brought US into war) • by air — dirigibles (e.g., German Zeppelin) and planes dropped bombs

Short Summary of Notes (Analysis):

Britain and her allies fought the Germans in Belgium and France after the German army invaded Belgium in 1914. Most of the fighting took place from trenches dug in places like Ypres and the Somme, but planes and dirigibles also dropped bombs. The Germans tried to stop supplies coming from North America by blowing up supply ships on their way to Britain. This brought the Americans into the war.

K-W-L: NOTE TAKING AND ORGANIZING INFORMATION

Topic: _____

Sources: _____

_____

K What I know about the topic	**W** What I want to learn about the topic	**L** What I learned about the topic

From D. Ogle, "A Teaching Model that Develops Active Reading of Expository Text," *The Reading Teacher* 59 (1986), 563–570.

COMPARE/CONTRAST CHART: TEMPLATE

Overall Topic: _____

Differences

Similarities

COMPARE/CONTRAST CHART: EXAMPLE

Overall Topic: Key individuals and events leading to Canadian confederation

Differences

Sir George-Étienne Cartier	Sir John A. Macdonald
• worked for French-Canadian interests within British parliamentary system, loyal to British	• Tory supporter who favoured business and railways and Anglican Church
• elected to the legislature as a Canada East member when 29 years old	• first elected to Legislative Assembly in 1844
• supported the 1837–1838 rebellion in Lower Canada and fled to the United States to avoid prison	• persuaded Liberals and Bleus to join to form the Liberal-Conservative Party in 1856
• leader of Le Parti Bleu	• wrote most of the 72 Resolutions of the British North America Act; presented these at the English Quebec Conference in 1864
• saw the new federation as a way of promoting better understanding	• chaired the London Conference in 1866

Similarities

- The Great Coalition with Cartier, Brown, and Macdonald was formed in 1864, ending coalition governments that lasted just months or even just days

- They both spoke at the Charlottetown meeting in 1864 about a federal system of government

- They both supported Confederation at the Quebec Conference in 1864

SAMPLE NOTES AND THOUGHTS

Topic: Alexander Graham Bell and His Inventions

Sources: MacLeod, E. *Alexander Graham Bell: An Inventive Life.* Toronto: Kids Can Press, 1999.
<www.pbs.org/wgbh/amex/telephone/peopleevents/mabell.html>

Notes	Thoughts
• born in Edinburgh, Scotland, in 1847	He was 23 years old when he moved with his family.
• both brothers died of tuberculosis and AGB was sick, so family moved to Ontario in 1870	
• his father created Visible Speech — symbols to help hearing-impaired communicate	His father was interested in sounds, too.
• AGB taught at Boston University as professor of vocal physiology and elocution	
• as a child experimented with system to collect rainwater and pipe it to the bathroom — his family now had a shower	He was inventing all the time and had a job as a professor. I wonder if he had time for any fun.
• tried to make a telegraph that could carry more than one message at a time	
• noticed that sound could make a metal disk vibrate, realized that sound could change electric currents	
• used a transmitter in offices in Brantford and Paris, Ontario, to send voice messages over the Dominion Telegraph Company lines	I wonder what I would say if I was having the first phone conversation. I think the people sang for 3 hours or something. I guess that's a good idea.
• married Mabel Hubbard, his deaf student, in 1877; they had two daughters	
• AGB had to fight 15 years in court to keep patent rights to telephone; others said they invented it first and he stole their ideas; AGB won	If AGB had lost the court case, I wouldn't be writing this report!
• AGB invented telephone probe to find bullet and save US President James Garfield when he was shot in 1881; the probe didn't save Garfield's life but did save other lives during WWI	
• invented audiometer, a device for testing hearing	He seemed to be curious about everything and trying to fix lots of problems.
• invented an air conditioning system	
• invented distilling devices for turning seawater into drinking water	
• invented tetrahedral kites for carrying people	
• worked with Aerial Experiment Association to design a plane, Silver Dart, that flew in 1909 (first plane to fly in Canada), after the Wright brothers flew their plane in 1903	
• built a hydrofoil (boat that travels over top of water); his "hydrodome" set a speed record of 112 km/h in 1919	It would have been fun to be his kids. They could fly and skim along the water in his inventions.
• AGB died in 1922 at 75; telephone service was stopped for one minute across North America during his funeral	That's a cool thing to do to honour AGB.

SAMPLE OUTLINE: ORGANIZING NOTES AND THOUGHTS ABOUT AGB

AGB's Life with his Family

- born in Edinburgh, Scotland, in 1847
- as a child, experimented with system to collect rainwater and pipe it to the bathroom (his family now had a shower)
- both brothers died of tuberculosis, and AGB was sick, so family moved to Ontario in 1870
- his father created Visible Speech—symbols to help hearing-impaired people communicate
- AGB taught at Boston University as professor of vocal physiology and elocution
- married Mabel Hubbard, his deaf student, in 1877; they had two daughters

Inventing the Telephone

- tried to make a telegraph that could carry more than one message at a time
- noticed that sound could make a metal disk vibrate; realized that sound could change electric currents
- used a transmitter in offices in Brantford and Paris, Ontario, to send voice messages over the Dominion Telegraph Company lines
- had to fight 15 years in court to keep patent rights to telephone; others said they invented it first and he stole their ideas; AGB won
- died in 1922 at 75; telephone service was stopped for one minute across North America during his funeral

Other Inventions

- invented telephone probe to find bullet and save US President James Garfield when he was shot in 1881; the probe didn't save Garfield's life but did save other lives during WWI
- invented audiometer, a device for testing hearing
- invented an air conditioning system
- invented distilling devices for turning seawater into drinking water
- invented tetrahedral kites for carrying people
- worked with Aerial Experiment Association to design a plane, Silver Dart, that flew in 1909 (first plane to fly in Canada) after the Wright brothers flew their plane in 1903
- built a hydrofoil (a boat that travels over the top of water); his "hydrodome" set a speed record of 112 km/h in 1919

PULLEYS USED TO RESCUE STRANDED WHALES

There was a large commotion last week at the coast near the town of Fake Lake. A large group of whales had been stranded on the shores of the lake.

This presented a problem of not enough space for patrons seeking an afternoon of fun in the sun. The bigger problem was that the rescue team had to return the whales to the water before they died.

They tried every idea that came to their mind, including pushing the whale with a tractor and offering the whale $50.00 to just get up and swim back into the water. All failed miserably. Time was running out when Pat Mercury, a concerned passerby, proposed that they implement a pulley system to lift and carry the whales to safety. Pat explained that a construction crane would do the work because cranes are designed to lift large amounts of weight.

The rescue workers hooked the whales and raised them one-by-one. They positioned the whales above a safe amount of water, lowered them into the water and detached the hoist. The whales were saved!

The rescue team was befuddled as to why they did not think of this earlier. If it were not for a knowledgeable stranger's assistance, the whales would surely have perished. With that in mind, the members of the rescue team resigned, sure that staying on duty would hurt more than help.

LEVERS FOR DUMMIES

What is a lever?

A lever is a simple machine. It consists of a rigid bar pivoted on a fixed point. A lever is used to transmit force, as in raising or moving a weight at one end by pushing down on the other.

How to use a lever

The lever is used for prying or lifting. There are three main parts to a lever. One part of a lever is a fulcrum. A fulcrum is known as the point on which the bar rests. The fulcrum lies between the effort and the load. Now, what is the effort arm? The part of the lever between the effort and the fulcrum is the effort arm. The part of the lever between the fulcrum and the load is the load arm.

First-class lever

Levers in which the fulcrum is located between the effort and the load are known as first-class levers. An example of a first-class lever is a see-saw.

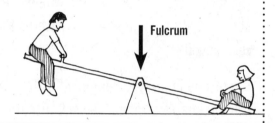

Second-class lever

When the fulcrum is located at one end of the lever with the effort applied at the other end and the load in between, it is called a second-class lever. Examples of a second-class lever are a wheelbarrow and a nutcracker.

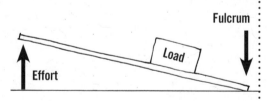

Third-class lever

The final possibility of a lever is known as a third-class lever. The effort is applied between the fulcrum and the load. An example of a third-class lever are tongs.

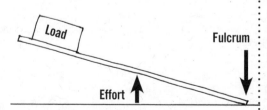

LOOKING AT INFORMATIONAL WRITING

Title

Overall idea
What is it?
How did the writer communicate this idea?

Key ideas
What are they?
How did you find the key ideas?

Supporting information
What are the supporting details?
How did the writer organize the writing to include supporting details?

ESTIMATING IN MATH IS A GOOD THING

My teachers told me that if I didn't estimate, I wouldn't be able to check to see if my answers made sense. **I didn't listen to them.** ☹ I used to think that estimating **was a waste of time**. I did my math questions as fast as I could so I wouldn't have homework. Who needs to round off big numbers to the nearest 10, 100, 1000, 10 000, and so on, and then add, multiply, subtract, or divide? Up until grade five, I didn't.

Then, in grade five, I had to do three pages of multiplication of two-digit by two-digit numbers, and some of them were decimal numbers. **I got almost all of them wrong!!!?** ☹ I put the decimals in the wrong places!!? My teacher told me that if I had estimated first, I would have known that the decimals were in the wrong places. I learned the hard way that **estimating is worth the little bit of time it takes**. Rounding numbers and figuring out whether the answer should be closer to 2000 than to 20 saves the horror of getting your work back with a whole bunch of X's on it. Believe me. **Estimating is a good thing!** ☺

LET'S KEEP ART

You will be surprised to hear that I think art is okay. I would much rather play soccer than draw, paint, or do any other art activity. Art is my worst class. Every time I try drawing or sculpting, it ends up being ugly. I would be happy to never have to take another art class. But there are people in my class who like art, so we shouldn't cut out art for everyone just because people like myself don't like it. Maybe some day I will like going to art galleries to see the paintings and sculptures. I like the posters in my room, so I already like some art. Maybe I'll even buy a painting some day.

We saw some Inuit soapstone sculptures at the museum last week. The narwhales with their long tusks looked vicious. Seeing those sculptures made me think about life as an Inuit. It would be hard work. If I hadn't seen the sculptures, I wouldn't know about Inuit. That's another good reason for having arts. They help to learn about different people. So even though I don't like doing art, I think that we should keep art. We'd miss art if we didn't have it.

LOOKING AT PERSUASIVE WRITING

Title

Writer's position What is it? How did the writer communicate his/her position?	Support for this position What supporting information did the writer include? How and where did the writer include this information?	Arguments against this position What are the arguments? How did the writer present opposing arguments and how did she/he deal with those opposing ideas?

DO YOU WANT TO STAY HEALTHY AND LIVE A LONG LIFE?

It's not hard to figure out what to do.

- Eat fruits and vegetables every day.

- Drink lots of water.

- Eat small amounts of meat, carbohydrates, and dairy products.

- Leave the junk food on the shelf at the store.

- Get enough sleep.

- Be active every day.

RECIPE FOR HEALTHY LIVING

4-5	servings fruit and vegetables		3-4	hours relaxation
2-3	servings carbohydrates (bread, cereal, rice, pasta)		1-2	hours physical activity
1-2	servings dairy products (milk, cheese, yoghurt)		1-2	hours laughter
1-2	servings protein (meat, beans)		5-6	hours hard work
6-8	glasses water		8-9	hours of sleep

Eat the fruit, carbohydrates, dairy products, and meat three times each day. Drink the water throughout the day, but not too much before you go to bed, or you won't get your 8-9 uninterrupted hours of sleep. Plan for some physical activity and relaxation each day. Work hard while you're at school so you learn lots. The laughter can happen any time (except in your sleep, of course!).

THINKING ABOUT WRITING THAT GIVES INSTRUCTIONS OR DIRECTIONS

Title	What do readers learn to do?	How are the ideas organized?	What kinds of words does the writer use to instruct or direct?

FIRST DRAFT: SOIL EROSION

Soil erosion is a bad thing. Soil erosion can be prevented by planting trees to make wind breaks and by leaving grass strips between plots of land that have been ploughed. It gets really dusty when farmers plough all the fields every year. All that dust goes into other people's yards.

Farm animals that eat the grass down to the dirt make it easier for soil to erode. These farm animals might be cows, sheep, or horses. Farmers plow the soil and make the dirt powdery. Powdery dirt blows in the wind and gets in your eyes. No one likes dust and no one likes soil erosion.

FINAL VERSION: SOIL EROSION AND HOW TO AVOID IT

Don't take soil for granted. It will not always be under your feet if you allow wind and rain to let it erode. Whenever it rains, the raindrops move soil. Whenever it is windy, the wind picks up the soil and moves it.

People make soil erode faster by doing certain things. When farmers allow cows, sheep and horses to eat the grass down to the dirt, or when they plow the soil too much so it's like powder, they make soil erosion happen faster. People who cut down all the trees on a hill make the soil looser so it will erode faster. Once soil is gone, plants have nothing to grow in.

We don't have to let that happen. Soil erosion can be prevented by planting trees to make wind breaks and by leaving grass strips between plots of land that have been ploughed. Plants and trees prevent soil erosion. They slow down rain water so that it soaks into the ground rather than pushing the soil along. The roots also hold the soil down so it can't be washed away.

Think about soil erosion whenever you dig up plants or trees or whenever you dig in the dirt. If you let the wind and rain wash all the soil away, what will be left of your back yard?

LIFE IN THE AMAZON BASIN WITH THE CABOCLOS AND THE SETTLERS—FIRST DRAFT

Two groups of people live in the Amazon basin: the Caboclos and the settlers. The Caboclos are different from the settlers. They grow different crops and travel in different ways.

They are the same because they both try to grow things on the land and end up causing environmental damage. The soil is poor, so it's hard for them to grow things. Life isn't easy in the Amazon basin for Caboclos or settlers.

COMPARE/CONTRAST CHART

Overall Topic: Notes taken from Waterlow, J. *The Amazon*. East Sussex, UK: Wayland, 1992.

Differences

Caboclos	Settlers
• European and Indian mixed race — have always lived there	• come from poorer areas with hope of creating a comfortable lifestyle for themselves
• live by the Amazon River — bananas are sold and transported by boat down the river	• settle beside roads because goods are transported by road
• catch fish and grow manioc and bananas	• raise cattle but pasture dies and weeds grow
• paddle on the river to go places	• clear land to grow cash crops
• like coffee	
• live in thatched-roof or corrugated-metal-roof homes	• population trebled between 1970 and 1980

Similarities

- live in Amazon basin
- crops can't be grown because of poor soil
- have to clear land frequently because soil is infertile
- long-lasting damage to the environment

USING QUOTES IN NON-NARRATIVE WRITING

How do I use quotes in my writing?

1. Summarize ideas or paraphrase what is written in print resources you use.

2. Explain your idea and then use a quote to help support that idea.

3. Make sure that any quote adds to what you want to say. Avoid using quotes just because they sound good.

4. Quotes are especially helpful when they come from someone who was an eyewitness to or took part in an event. If you are writing a biography, for example, use quotes from the person you are writing about to give readers a better sense of what the person was/is like.

How should I incorporate quotes into my writing?

1. Always use quotation marks "..." to enclose the words that are quoted.

2. In parentheses, write the last name of the original writer, the year that the text was published, and the page number where you found the quote. For example: (Smith 2005, 10)

3. You can start a sentence with your own idea and finish it with the quote.

4. You can start a sentence with the name of the original author followed by a verb such as "states," "explains," or "writes." Put the quote in quotation marks.

5. The sentences before and after the quote should relate to the quote. In fact, the sentence following the quote should explain parts of it or show how the quote fits in with your idea. It explains why you used the quote.

6. Try to use as few words from the original source as possible. A good guideline is to use no more than three sentences. This will vary. Remember, lengthy quotes break up the flow of the writing and sometimes steer the writing away from your own ideas.

ONE STUDENT'S USE OF QUOTES

How Coffee and Doughnuts Mix with Hockey: The Story of Tim Hortons

Tim Horton was a defenseman who started playing in the NHL in 1952 with the Toronto Maple Leafs. He was known as "the strongest man ever to lace up skates in the National Hockey League" (Hockey Hall of Fame and Museum, 2001-2003, unpaginated). Montreal Canadien John Ferguson knew how tough Horton was. He said, "Horton's the hardest bodychecker I've ever come up against. He's as strong as an ox and hits with terrific force" (Shea, 2003, unpaginated). The Leafs won four Stanley Cups while Horton played with them. In 1969, he was traded to the New York Rangers, then to the Pittsburgh Penguins, and finally to the Buffalo Sabres. In 1973, he was named the Sabres' Most Valuable Player at the age of 43.

Tim Horton realized that he could not gain financial security through his hockey income. He and his partner, Jim Charade, opened hamburger restaurants that were unsuccessful before they had the idea to sell coffee and doughnuts. Tim Horton continued to play hockey as more and more doughnut stores opened up.

On February 21, 1974, Tim Horton was killed in a car crash driving back to Buffalo after playing a game in Toronto. He was driving the sports car that the Sabres had given him as a bonus for signing that year. Tim Horton was recognized for his hockey playing, as he entered the Hockey Hall of Fame in 1977. His name is known by hockey fans and doughnut eaters, as there are 2000 or more stores bearing his name. Jamie Fitzpatrick (2005, unpaginated) says that because of his coffee shops, "Tim Horton ranks with Henderson, Howe, Orr, Hull, Richard and Number 99 as one of Canada's most famous hockey players."

References

Fitzpatrick, J. *Tim Horton: Hockey Legend and Fast Food Icon*, 2005. <http://proicehockey.about.com/od/history/a/tim_horton.htm>

Hockey Hall of Fame and Museum (2001-2003). *Tim Horton*. <www.legendsofhockey.net:8080/LegendsOfHockey/jsp/LegendsMember.jsp?mem=p197702andtype=Playerandpage=bioandlist>

Shea, K. *One on One with Tim Horton*, 2003. <www.legendsofhockey.net/html/spot_oneononep197702.htm>

GRAPHIC DESIGN: THINGS YOU CAN DO

Lines and White Space

- Separate graphics and text by drawing a line across or down a page.

- Highlight and separate text or graphics by drawing boxes around them.

- Give readers' eyes a break by leaving lots of white space around the text and graphics.

Font

- Emphasize words, titles, headings, or phrases using:

  bold type   ALL CAPS   *italics*

  <u>underlining</u>   larger type size

- Convey the tone or mood of your writing through the font:

  Times New Roman   a formal typeface used in books and newspapers

  Andy   a less formal typeface that looks like carefree printing

  AvantGarde   a bold font that works well for headings

  Arial   a fairly formal font that is easy to read

Heading and Subheadings

Usually, headings work in levels:

The First Level Is Usually the Title of Your Writing.
It Stands Out by Being Centred and is often ALL CAPS or
In Larger Font Size. It May Be **Bold** or <u>Underlined</u>.

Second-Level Headings Stand Apart from the Paragraphs that Follow Them,
Usually by Being in Title Case and/or by Being Centred. They may be underlined.

Third-level headings also stand apart from the paragraphs that follow them. Usually they are flush with the left margin. <u>They may be underlined.</u>

SENTENCES THAT CAN BE USED FOR MAKING LINE BREAKS

Experiment with line breaks as you create a poem from this statement:

Mountains can make the weather wetter—or drier—in one area than in nearby areas. When warm, moist winds sweep up the sides of mountains, clouds form, and rain falls. On the other side of the mountains it may be desert-like. (Wyatt and Share 2000, p. 7).

V. Wyatt and B. Share, *Weather*, Toronto: Kids Can Press, 2000.

TWO EXAMPLES OF THE USE OF LINE BREAKS

How do the two poems below give you a different impression of the effect of mountains on weather? Which words are emphasized in each one? What do you do differently when you read each poem aloud? What makes you read them differently?

Example 1
Mountains can make the weather wetter —
or drier —
than nearby areas.
When warm, moist winds
sweep up the sides of a mountain,
clouds form,
and rain falls. On the other side
of the mountain
it may be desert-like.

Example 2
Mountains
can make the weather wetter — or drier —
than nearby areas.
When warm, moist winds
sweep
up the side of a mountain,
clouds form
and rain falls.
On the other side of the mountain
it may be
desert-like.

ASHIF'S NOTES FROM A WEBSITE AND PRESENTATION FROM HEALTH NURSE

Topic: Harmful effects of smoking

Sources: <www.cancer.org/docroot/PED/ped_10_1.asp?sitearea=PED>
Health Nurse presentation

Notes	Thoughts
• Each year, nearly 1 of every 5 deaths in USA related to smoking. About 87% of lung cancer deaths caused by smoking. Smoking causes heart disease, lung, larynx, oral, esophagus, bladder, and pancreas cancer.	• If everyone quit smoking, there would be a lot more people still alive.
• Tobacco products contain nicotine. Nicotine is addictive and poisonous. More than 60 compounds that cause cancer are found in cigarettes — include ammonia, tar, and carbon monoxide.	• Why would anyone want to take something that is poisonous?
• Carbon monoxide is emitted (400 times greater than what is considered safe in industrial settings). Carbon monoxide interferes with ability of blood to transport oxygen to body.	• So that's why people who smoke have a hard time running and climbing stairs and stuff.
• In 1988, the US Surgeon General said that being addicted to nicotine is like being addicted to drugs such as heroin or cocaine.	• My uncle has been smoking for 35 years. He says he can't quit. He's addicted.

Repeated sounds:

nicotine	addictive	smoking	heart disease
needles	admire	sorry	heart-stopping
magazine	active	swimming	please
been	address	smile	harm
tobacco	oxygen	carbon monoxide	cancer
tempo	odd	cartoon	sir
toast	again	messes	candy
whacko	auditorium	carry	candle

In his poem, Ashif used a few of the words from his list. He liked the sound of the word *nicotine* and decided to repeat it.

SMOKE AND YOU'LL BE SORRY!

Tobacco has nicotine, nicotine,
Don't know it's addictive —
Where have you been?

Smoking is harmful.
You'll get heart disease and cancer.
Yes sir,
The carbon monoxide messes up
Blood carrying oxygen.
Don't make me say it again.

Tobacco has nicotine, nicotine.
And it is addictive —
You know what I mean!

WATER BUGS IN MY NOTEBOOK: SHELBI'S SCIENCE POEM

I went to a pond with my class
to put water bugs in my notebook
My teacher said
write everything you see
in the pond.

And so I did.

I saw a water strider
with long legs
like pole vaults with hinges
walking on top of the water.
It left a dimple in the water

Where it stepped.

I saw a round black
backswimmer
moving away from its head
with quick, short back strokes.

The water strider didn't pay attention
To the backswimmer
And the backswimmer ignored
The water strider.

I was the only one
Paying attention to both of them.

SMUDGEY FUN IN ART CLASS: RATIBA'S ART POEM

Crayons slide on paper
like skates on ice.
Not a cloud in the sky Blue.
is my favourite colour.
I used it a lot to draw kites.

My hand rubbed on the kites
accidentally
and they had
blue tails in funny places.
Blue smudges on the pink flowers
and the kids flying the kites.

Today I used pastels in art.

LIST POEM ON MEDIA IMAGES OF GIRLS CREATED FROM OVERHEAD TRANSPARENCY STRIPS

Students write list poems about differences between "real life" girls or boys and those portrayed in the media to gain a better understanding of how the media influences body image.

Two fifth-grade girls wrote these poems:

Magazine Ad Girls	**Real Life Girls**
Don't eat much,	Sometimes eat too much,
Are very skinny,	Sometimes go on diets,
Wear designer clothes,	Can be all sorts of sizes,
Have cute faces,	Are cute in their own way,
Don't have zits.	Pop zits every other day.

WE HELPED BRING CONFEDERATION TO CANADA

Voice of Sir George-Étienne Cartier

Voice of Sir John A. Macdonald

I am French Canadian.

I am a Scottish immigrant.

I supported the Lower Canada
rebellion and fled to the USA.

I supported business, railways,
and the Anglican Church.

We were elected to the legislature.

I'm Canada East.

I'm Canada West.

Heard of the Great Coalition? That was us (and George Brown).

New federation? It's great for better
understanding between French
and English

New federation? I wrote 72 Resolutions

Charlottetown, Quebec, London. We were there 1864 to 1866.
Confederation Rocks!

DISTILLING A POEM FROM A PARAGRAPH

The homes of animals are always changing. Some changes happen in nature, and others are caused by people. When an animal's habitat, or living area, is no longer the same, that animal must adapt, or change, to suit its new habitat. (Kalman, 2000, p. 4).

Why Do Animals Adapt?
Animal homes
(or habitats)
Are always changing.
Sometimes nature is the cause,
Sometimes people are.
Animals change
To suit their new habitat.

B. Kalman, *How Do Animals Adapt?* St. Catharines, ON: Crabtree Publishing, 2000.

EXAMPLE OF A POEM CREATED FROM A LIST OF GEOMETRY WORDS

List of words for geometry unit:

square	slurp	construct	congruent	frying pan
trapezoid	hockey	translate	symmetrical	pizza
line	elbow	rotate	parallel	marshmallow
rectangle	burn	draw	three-dimensional	howling

Here is the poem created by a grade-4 class:

Hockey Rinks are Rectangles for a Reason

We tried to construct
a trapezoid hockey rink
yesterday.
Scoring goals is harder—
The sides are not congruent.
You go deeper in the corner
On one side
With the defense's elbows
Holding you back.

Where do we draw the blue line?
How do we set up the goals
across from each other?
Only two sides are parallel.

Trapezoid hockey rinks
Get hockey players howling.

MECHANICAL ADVANTAGE HAUNTS YOU

Jim was a very lazy and ignorant kid. "Who needs mechanical advantage!" he would always say. Of course, this always made his life harder, especially since he wasn't that strong himself. Soon he began to forget what mechanical advantage really was, and was simply lost in a world of hard work. He couldn't keep up with it, and his laziness only made matters worse. It seemed that there was no hope left for this poor soul. Fortunately for him, though, he was being watched. And hope would come sooner than he thought. One night he fell asleep, but right after he fell asleep, he found himself sitting on his bed.

"Ah, this is one odd dream," he said to himself. He turned around to see himself or what seemed to be his "body," sleeping on his bed.

"OK, this is getting weird," he said. It would soon get weirder, for a shadowy figure emerged out of nowhere. Jim couldn't help letting out a high, girlish cry for help.

"Silence!" said the figure.

"I, the Ghost of Pulleys have appeared before you today to teach you a lesson. I am one of the three Ghosts of Mechanical Advantage. You have been very foolish lately, being ignorant about the power of mechanical advantage! Prepare to be educated!" Jim was quickly sucked into what seemed to be … a science classroom? There, standing in front of him was the Ghost of Pulleys.

"Now, it is time for your enlightenment. The pulley can greatly help you be reducing the force needed to lift an object." Jim slowly but surely began to understand how helpful pulleys were. Moveable pulleys, fixed pulleys, double pulleys, the works.

"So, the more sections of rope I have, the easier it is to lift?" Jim asked.

"Of course," replied the ghost.

After an adequate lesson with the Ghost of Pulleys, Jim was sent to the next ghost. A swirling vortex opened up before him and he jumped in. Whoosh! Jim landed in a playground where he saw a see-saw in the middle, and a bunch of other things lying around, such as a hockey stick, a pair of shears, a hammer, and a crowbar.

"Alas, the uneducated mortal has arrived," sounded a booming voice.

"Let me guess," Jim replied. "The Ghost of Levers."

The ghost was very pleased, "Ah, that gets a lot of things out of the way. Now, it is time for your enlightenment." Jim was told about Class 1, Class 2 and Class 3 levers, as well as how you can find them in real life.

"Yes, levers can help you greatly when used correctly. Now for your final destination." The vortex appeared before Jim again and he jumped in, wondering what was next. Tick-tock, tick-tock, tick-tock.

"Where am I?" Jim said in exasperation. His surroundings were quite different from the last two. First the classroom, then the playground, but now… inside a clock tower? There were gears everywhere, all kinds of gears, all working together to make the clock precisely accurate. Suddenly, a shadowy figure leaped out from behind one of the gears. "Howdy there, partner! You ready for some gear education?"

"Sure, I'm guessing the Gear Ghost, right?" replied Jim.

"Right you are," said the ghost.

The ghost quickly launched him to the top of the tower and proceeded to explain all about gears: driver gears, follower gears, even rack-and-pinion gears. At the end of his lesson with the gear ghost, a vortex appeared and sucked him in without warning. After a couple of seconds, he was quickly sent to his room and returned to the position he was in before on the bed. In front of him were the three ghosts.

The Ghost of Pulleys stepped forward, took a deep breath, and said, "Use the knowledge you have just learned to assist you in daily life." Then the Ghost of Levers stepped forward and said, "Do not forget what we have taught you."

And finally the Ghost of Gears stepped forward and said, "I reckon we could do this again sometime. We'll be here if you're ever in need." The three ghosts quickly huddled together, and, before you could say "mechanical advantage," they disappeared.

Jim sighed and then climbed into his bed. "Wow," he said, "I really need to lay off the junk food."

THE CASE OF THE MISSING BABY

Detective Starling sat in her office. She was about to leave when suddenly a lady walked into her office. "My baby is gone! Please find her for me. She's my only child!" Starling could see that this lady was really upset. "Don't worry, lady. I'll find your baby for you," she said. The lady gave Starling her address and then walked out of her office.

Starling went to the lady's house. She knocked on the door and asked where the baby was when it had been kidnapped. The lady showed Starling to the basement. She looked around and then she found an open window. Under the window she found a metal box and some gears. She opened the back of the box and put the gears on some nails that were inside the box. As Starling began turning one of the gears, the other gears began turning, too. A huge bang came out of the box and then a note flew out of the box. On the note was written:

IF YOU EVER WANT TO SEE YOUR BABY COME TO THE OLD FACTORY AT MIDNIGHT AND BRING TWO HUNDRED THOUSAND DOLLARS WITH YOU. DON'T TRY ANYTHING FUNNY OR ELSE...

THIS NOTE WAS WRITTEN BY:
DR. LEVER

Starling had no other choice but to go to the factory.

Starling walked into the dark factory. She came earlier than midnight so that she could set some traps.

She looked around and found an old piece of wood and some bricks. She put eight bricks at the bottom and then put the piece of wood on top of them. Starling then went to look for something heavy to put on top of the inclined plane. The only thing she could find was an old TV. She pushed it up the piece of wood. It was easier to do than she had thought.

Next, Starling found an old flagpole. She took one end of the rope on the flagpole's pulley and tied it around a nearby box. She took the other end of the rope and made a circle with it.

Midnight came and Starling thought that no one would come. Then, she heard some footsteps. They were getting closer and closer. She decided that it was time to use her first trap. When she thought that Dr. Lever was close enough, she pushed the TV off the inclined plane. She heard someone go, "OUCH!!!" She hoped that the baby had not been hurt.

She then ran to the flagpole and held on to the end she had tied to the box. She waited until the kidnapper's foot was in the right place. She pulled on the end of the pulley. The other end went up and she could feel some weight on it. She had caught the kidnapper! The baby had escaped from Dr. Lever when he was hit by the TV. The police came and arrested Dr. Lever and the baby was returned to her mother.

And so, the case was solved thanks to Starling's quick thinking and her grade-eight science teacher, who taught her everything she knows about levers, gears and pulleys!

LIFE IN ANCIENT GREECE

"Pericles, your father is waiting for you," his mother warned. Don't make him late for the Assembly."

Pericles ran to the door. Clutching his leather hoop and clay ball. He closed the door of their sun-dried brick house and stepped into the street. This was the first time he was going to his cousin's new house. His father said Pericles could play with his cousin all day while his father was at the assembly where citizens debated and passed laws.

Pericles trotted beside his father he noticed all the women with slaves as their chaperones. Soon they were in the market. Suddenly, he saw a man whipping the slave who sold fish in his stall. He stopped to watch what was happening. Not noticing that his father had kept walking.

"That's the last time you'll run away from me, Pandora. I don't know why I bring you to market. From now on, I'll keep you locked up in the house doing housework," the man cried as he whipped Pandora hard along her back.

Pericles looked around to tell his father that they should do something to help. But he only saw peasant farmers selling food from the land they had inherited or got as a reward for serving in the military.

"Great," thought Pericles, now how am I supposed to get to my cousins house?"

He saw Pandora looking defiantly at her owner. She threw a fish on the table peasant woman to buy. Her owner turned around to serve the woman and Pandora ran as fast as she could into the crowd. Pericles watched her dart behind a cart piled high with olives.

"Where did she go?" her owner roared.

"She went in that direction, sir," Pericles pointed in the opposite direction. The man lumbered of. He left the unfree labourer. Who worked to pay off a debt he owed the man to sell the fish.

Suddenly, Pericles' father was standing over him. "So you've been standing here all along, Pericles. Why didn't you follow me? I was almost out of the market before I realized you weren't beside me."

"Sorry father," Pericles said. "I was watching some people. I should have stayed closer to you."

Pandora watched everything that happened. She nodded to Pericles as he and his father walked past the cart she was hiding behind. Then she walked off to a new life. She was no longer a slave because her owner never found her again.

DEVELOPING CHARACTERS

What are their names?			
What roles do they play in the story? (e.g., protagonist, sister/brother/ friend of protagonist, villain)			
How do they stand out from others?			
What are their goals/problems/ motivations?			
Do they have physical features/ gestures/facial expressions that are unique? What are they?			
What personalities do they have? What are their strengths? What are their weaknesses?			

HOW AUTHORS USE DIALOGUE IN NARRATIVES

Instructions: Read the dialogue aloud with a friend, taking on the roles of the characters. Then complete the chart for each conversation you read.

Title of story	Kind of information the dialogue provides	Words and expressions that seem natural	What is written before and after the dialogue	Number of lines of dialogue	Number of characters involved	How often the speaker's name is attached to the dialogue	"Said" words

DETAILS TO ADD TO A SENTENCE

Add details to the following:

Winter was hard for Chu. _____

_____

_____

_____

_____

_____

_____

_____

_____

Paul Yee's Details

Then winter came and halted all work. Snows buried everything under a heavy blanket of white. The white boss went to town to live in a warm hotel, but Chu and the workers stayed in camp. The men tied potato sacks around their feet and huddled by the fire, while ice storms howled like wolves through the mountains. Chu thought winter would never end. ("Spirit of the Railway" in *Deadman's Gold and Other Stories.* Toronto: Groundwood, 2002, p.13.)

CUTTING EXCESSIVE DETAILS

Cut unnecessary information:

The crew put up their tents very quickly so they could get to work. They tried to find a level spot to lay out the black ground sheets. They needed hammers to pound in the tent pegs. Many of the pegs were bent, and the tents had a lot of holes. The men worried that their blankets would get wet in the rain. They didn't like the white bosses telling them what to do all the time. Chu thought the white bosses were mean. He felt like talking back to them, but knew he would get into trouble if he did. The men worked very hard and didn't talk to each other.

Then, all of the tents were up, and it was time to go to work. They had to make a pathway for the trains that would be steaming through some day. The men knew they might never be rich enough to ride the trains, but they hoped their children would be able to ride them some day. Chu and the other men climbed a hill and started working away at scooping out the dirt to make a path. They used picks to loosen the rocks and tree roots. Then they scooped the rocks and roots up with shovels. They threw the rocks and roots down the side of the mountain, grunting with the effort. It was hard work, and they didn't get paid very much for it. But at least things weren't all that expensive, like they are today, so they could still save some money to send to their families in China. They had sore arms after a few hours, but they kept working.

Paul Yee's Details

The crew pitched their tents and began to work. They hacked at hills with hand-scoops and shovels to level a pathway for the train. Their hammers and chisels chipped boulders into gravel and fill. Their dynamite and drills thrust tunnels deep into the mountain. At night, the crew would sit around the campfire chewing tobacco, playing cards and talking. ("Spirit of the Railway" in *Deadman's Gold and Other Stories.* Toronto: Groundwood, 2002, p.12.)

BEGINNINGS AND ENDINGS: QUESTIONS TO CONSIDER

Title of Book: _____

Beginning (Lead)

- What did the author do (e.g., introduce characters, introduce setting)?

Ending

- Did the main character solve the problem himself/herself or get help from others?

- What questions did the ending answer? What questions (if any) did the ending leave unanswered?

- Did the main character go back to ordinary life, or did she/he move on to another setting?

- Did the main character change in any way? How did she/he change?

WHAT *IT'S* OR *ITS* REPLACES

Directions: Read the poem about states of matter, noting where *its* and *it's* appear. Write what other words you could use instead of *its* and *it's* in each line. The first two have been coupled as examples for you.

Three States of Matter

It's all about   It is
temperature and pressure.

Increase temperature or
pressure
on a solid.
Its molecules move faster –   The solid's
It's becoming a liquid.

Or,
on a liquid.
Its molecules move faster –
It's becoming a gas.

Ice is a solid.
Its molecules stay put.
Ice holds its shape.

Water is a liquid.
Its molecules move a little
and take the shape of *its* container.

Water vapour is a gas.
Its molecules bounce around
to fill all available space.

Add or take away
energy.
It's what you do to change
states of matter.

I am a solid,
But I exhale air.
And there's liquid blood in my veins.

Follow up: What is the difference in meaning between *its* and *it's*? How will you remember the difference?

INVESTIGATING AUTHORS' USES OF COMMAS

Find examples of the way commas are used in books and magazines. Then look at all the examples in each category, and come up with a rule that explains how the authors have used commas and why you think they used them in this way.

Category 1: Lists of actions or things

Examples: _____

_____

_____

What seems to be the rule for using commas? _____

_____

_____

Category 2: Dialogue

Examples: _____

_____

_____

What seems to be the rule for using commas? _____

_____

_____

Category 3: When there are dates and years

Examples: _____

_____

_____

What seems to be the rule for using commas? _____

_____

_____

Category 4: When there are names of towns, cities, provinces, countries, and states

Examples: _____

_____

_____

What seems to be the rule for using commas? _____

_____

_____

Category 5: Separating clauses (e.g., There are two clauses in this sentence; one is underlined and the other is italicized: <u>After the students looked for commas in books and magazines</u>, *they figured out the rules for using commas*.)

Examples: _____

_____

_____

What seems to be the rule for using commas? _____

_____

_____

Your Category: In what other ways do authors use commas? Write three or more examples that do not fit any of the other categories, and figure out a rule to explain what the commas are used for.

Examples: _____

_____

_____

What seems to be the rule for using commas? _____

_____

_____

EDITING AND PROOFREADING ONE STUDENT'S WRITING

Directions: Read the following dialogue, and identify where the writer has used commas correctly. Think about the rules that the writer has correctly followed in his use of commas. Circle the unnecessary commas—those that get in the way of understanding the sentence. Write a comma in the places where you feel commas are needed to make the meaning clearer.

Celine sat up, stretched and slowly got ready for school. She had cereal, orange juice a grapefruit and toast for breakfast.

"You're going to miss the bus" , her mom warned.

"No, the bus driver always waits for me."

"Pass the milk please." That was Raymond, Celine's brother, talking.

He reached across the table because everyone was ignoring him.

"If the two of you would get out of bed when I called you, then you wouldn't have to rush through your breakfast," Celine's mom said.

"You move so slowly that you will probably get to school by November 30, 2020", said Raymond to his sister.

"At least I don't have my shirt on inside out like you do," Celine retorted.

"That's enough, you two. I'm going to ship you off to your grandmother's in Tokyo Japan if I don't see you rushing out that door. Maybe she'll be able to get you moving in the morning."

Celine and Raymond streaked past her to the bus as it pulled up in the laneway.

PROOFREADING THE "HOW TO BE A GOOD FRIEND" QUIZ

Their are lots of things you can do to be a good friend. I (no) what I'm talking about. I have more friends than (enyone) I know.

Here is a quiz to teach you how to be the best (freind) you can be. Choose the best (ansewr) you can find. The (write) answers are at the bottom of this page. Good luck! I hope you have fun (makeing) new friends!

1. When (you're) lab partner in (scince) class thinks you should build a tower with Popsicle sticks and you think it should be built with toothpicks, what should you do?

    A.   Tell that person to jump in a lake.

    B.   Be open-minded and discuss the situation. You might have to compromise and use some Popsicle sticks and some toothpicks.

2. When someone on your soccer team is being told (bye) other kids that he or she is ugly, what should you do?

    A.   Stick up for the person (buy) telling the other kids to leave her or him alone.

    B.   Join in and tell the person that she or he is uglier than a (wharthog.)

Correct:

1. B

2. A

EDITING SYMBOLS

Insert	∧	Insert exclamation mark	
Insert comma		Insert question mark	
Insert apostrophe		Insert period	
Insert quotation marks		Delete	
Capitalize	a̲	Change to lower case	/lc
Check spelling	sp	Indent	→
Transpose (change the order)	tr	New paragraph	⁋or¶

USING EDITING SYMBOLS

Directions: Proofread the following letter by using editing symbols to show this grade-5 student what she needs to do to improve her writing.

Dear Editor

I think people are driving to much and using up to much gasoline. Gasoline is a non-renewable resources. Non-renewable resources produce carbon dioxide. Which is changing the climate. Have you ever breathed in car exhaust. It stinks right? Thats pollusion. Another problem is that gasoline will run out some day. I like being able to drive with my parents to basketball games, like everyone else. But the gas that our car burns cant be used agian. If we use all the gas in the world there won't be gas for future generations to drive they're kids to basketball games We should start car pooling and riding our bikes. If we live in a city, we should take a bus or the subway. All of these things will conserve gas for the future.

Yours truly,

A. Singh

Grade five student

PRACTISE USING EDITING SYMBOLS

Directions: Proofread this essay by using editing symbols to show this writer what he needs to do to improve his writing.

The Life of Ray Charles, Father of Soul Music

Ray Charles Robinson was born September 23, 1930, in Georgia. He had a terrible thing happen to him when he was just five years old he saw his brother drown in a large laundry tub. You have all seen pictures of Ray charles as an adult and know he was blind. Did you know that he was blind bye the time he was seven years old

Ray learned to read write and arrange music in Braille, and play piano organ, saxophone, clarinet and trumpet at a school for the deaf and blind. He started touring the south with dance bands that played in black dance halls. He dropped his last name to avoid confusion with the boxer, Sugar ray robinson. He developed his own style of music. It was like gospel music. With hoots and hollers and non-religious words. He made a hit record in 1954 called "I Got a Woman." This was the begining of a new type of music called Soul.

In February 1958, he recorded a song that sold over a million records called "What'd I Say." In 1961, "Hit the Road Jack" won one of his 12 Grammy awards. Ray Charles also made country music records that were very populer. In 1964 he was arrested. After customs officers found drugs in his coat. Ray Charles took a year off from touring to kick his drug addiction. In 1966 he was given a five-year suspended sentence for drug possession. Ray Charles died on June 10 2004, at the age of 73.

NOTES FROM STUDENT-TEACHER CONFERENCES

Students' Names and Dates of Conference			

ASSESSING CONTENT AREA WRITING: CHECKLIST

Content   **Points out of** ____

1. Provides information about all concepts   _____

2. Provides accurate information about concepts so it is easy to see
    that the writer understands the concepts   _____

3. Creates a context that presents a thoughtful and perhaps new way
    of looking at the concept   _____

4. Provides specific supporting details consistently so the writing
    is easy to understand and creative/engaging   _____

5. Consistently shows connections among the concepts   _____

6. Maintains a clear focus   _____

7. Uses multiple sources of information   _____

8. Tries out new ideas or perspectives and/or writes against stereotypes _____

Organization

1. Uses an appropriate beginning and ending to identify clearly
    what writer is trying to achieve   _____

2. Uses the structure of the genre to achieve the student's purpose _____

3. Organizes ideas in a way that contributes to the intended effect on readers _____

Style

1. Uses language and design appropriate for the audience and genre _____

2. Uses specific words and expressions, and a variety of sentence structures /
    line breaks / graphic design in a creative and effective way   _____

3. Uses a variety of sentence structures / line breaks / graphics in a
    creative and effective way   _____

4. Chooses graphics and formats that further the writer's purpose _____

5. Puts graphics and text together in ways that achieve the desired
    purpose or effect on readers   _____

Conventions

1. Consistently and effectively uses spelling, grammar, and punctuation appropriate
    to the social context   _____

                                                        Total _____

ASSESSING CONTENT AREA POETRY WRITING: CHECKLIST

Content
Points out of _____

1. Provides information about all the concepts _____

2. Provides accurate information about the concepts so it is easy to see that the writer understands the concepts _____

3. Creates a context that presents a thoughtful and perhaps new way of looking at the concept _____

4. Provides specific supporting details consistently so the writing is easy to understand and creative/engaging _____

5. Consistently shows connections among the concepts _____

6. Uses multiple sources of information _____

7. Says a lot with few words _____

8. If titles are used, they contribute to the overall meaning _____

9. Tries out new ideas or perspectives and/or writes against stereotypes _____

Organization

1. Ideas flow smoothly and are easy to follow _____

2. Line breaks add to the meaning and make the poem easy to follow _____

Style

1. Creates images through one or more of the senses _____

2. Plays with rhythms and sounds of language _____

3. Uses repetition to emphasize ideas or add to the rhythm of the poem _____

4. Chooses media that further the writer's purpose _____

5. Puts graphics and text together in ways that achieve the desired purpose or effect on readers _____

Conventions

1. Consistently and effectively uses correct spelling, grammar, and punctuation appropriate for the situation _____

Total _____

ASSESSING CONTENT AREA NARRATIVE WRITING: CHECKLIST

Content

Points out of ____

1. Provides information about all the concepts _____

2. Provides accurate information about all the concepts so it is clear that the writer understands the concepts _____

3. Creates a context that presents a thoughtful and perhaps new way of looking at the concept _____

4. Supporting details enhance character development, setting, and plot. The writing is easy to understand and creative/engaging _____

5. Consistently shows connections among the concepts _____

6. Uses multiple sources of information _____

7. Dialogue is natural, develops character, and moves plot forward _____

8. Content information is woven into the writing in a way that does not disrupt the flow of the story _____

9. Story has a clear focus and is easy to follow _____

10. Tries out new ideas or perspectives and/or writes against stereotypes _____

Organization

1. Story events and ideas flow, are clearly connected and are easy to follow _____

2. Lead provides sufficient information to bring readers into the story in an engaging way _____

3. Satisfying ending ties events together _____

4. Organizes ideas in a way that contributes to the intended effect on readers _____

Style

1. Specific words and expressions engage readers _____

2. Uses a variety of simple, compound, and complex sentences _____

3. Chooses media that further the writer's purpose _____

4. Puts graphics and text together in ways that achieve the desired purpose or effect on readers _____

Conventions

1. Consistently and effectively uses correct spelling, grammar, and punctuation appropriate to the situation _____

Total _____

ASSESSING CONTENT AREA NON-NARRATIVE WRITING: CHECKLIST

Content

Points out of ____

1. Provides information about all the concepts

   _____

2. Provides accurate information about the concepts so it is clear that the writer understands them

   _____

3. Creates a context that presents a thoughtful and perhaps new way of looking at the concept

   _____

4. Provides specific supporting details consistently so the writing is easy to understand and creative/engaging

   _____

5. Consistently shows connections among the concepts

   _____

6. Uses multiple sources of information and includes references

   _____

7. Tries out new ideas or perspectives and/or writes against stereotypes

   _____

Organization

1. Uses an appropriate beginning and ending to identify clearly what the writer is trying to achieve

   _____

2. Uses the structure of the genre to achieve the writer's purpose

   _____

3. Organizes ideas in a way that contributes to the intended effect on readers

   _____

Style

1. Uses language appropriate for the audience and genre

   _____

2. Uses specific words and expressions, and a variety of sentence structures to achieve the writer's purpose

   _____

3. Chooses graphics and formats that further the writer's purpose

   _____

4. Puts graphics and text together in ways that achieve the desired purpose or effect on readers

   _____

Conventions

1. Consistently and effectively uses spelling, grammar, and punctuation appropriate to the situation

   _____

Total   _____